WUQIA

KUCHE

TURFAN

XINJIANG

GANSU

JIAYUGUAN

QINGHAI

XINING

XIZANG
(TIBET)

SICHUAN

YUANMOU
YUNNAN

0   300km

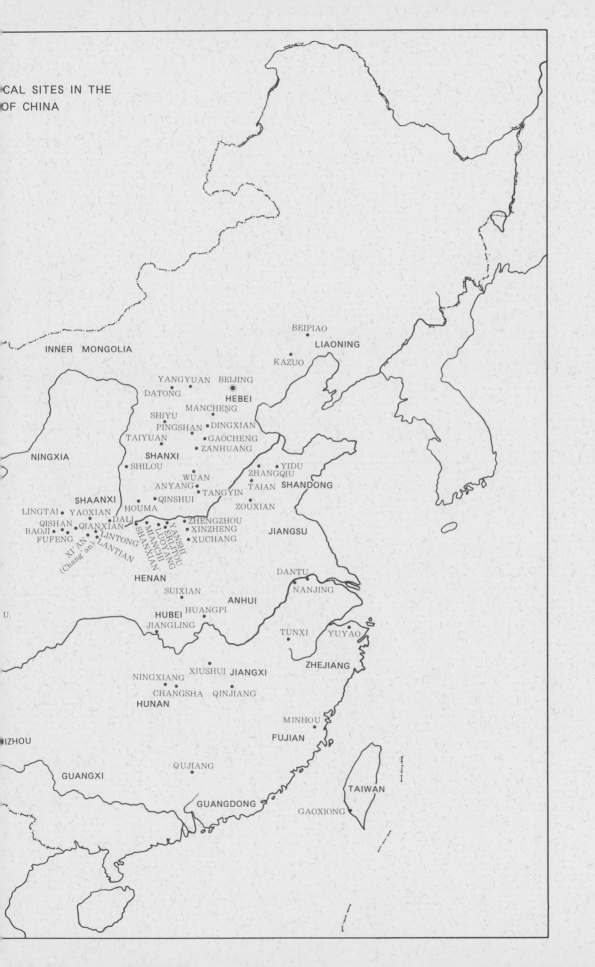

CAL SITES IN THE
OF CHINA

INNER MONGOLIA

BEIPIAO
LIAONING
KAZUO

YANGYUAN BEIJING
DATONG HEBEI
MANCHENG
SHIYU
PINGSHAN DINGXIAN
TAIYUAN GAOCHENG
ZANHUANG
NINGXIA SHANXI
SHILOU
YIDU
ZHANGQIU
WUAN
ANYANG TAIAN SHANDONG
SHAANXI TANGYIN
QINSHUI
HOUMA ZOUXIAN
LINGTAI YAOXIAN
QISHAN QIANXIAN DALI ZHENGZHOU JIANGSU
BAOJI XINZHENG
FUFENG LINTONG XUCHANG
XI'AN LANTIAN
(Chang'an)
YANSHI
ERLITOU
LUOYANG
MANCHI
SHANXIAN
DANTU
HENAN NANJING
SUIXIAN
ANHUI
HUANGPI
HUBEI
JIANGLING TUNXI YUYAO

ZHEJIANG
XIUSHUI JIANGXI
NINGXIANG
CHANGSHA QINJIANG
HUNAN
MINHOU
IZHOU FUJIAN

QUJIANG
GUANGXI TAIWAN

GUANGDONG
GAOXIONG

Recent Archaeological Discoveries

in

The People's Republic of China

XIA NAI (夏鼐) was born in 1910. He is Honorary Director of the Institute of Archaeology at the Chinese Academy of Social Sciences and Vice-President of the Chinese Academy of Social Sciences. He participated in excavations at Anyang in China in 1935 and Maiden Castle in England in 1936. He has supervised many excavations in China. He received a Ph.D. in Egyptology from the University of London. He is a Correspondent Fellow of the British Academy and of the German Archaeological Institute, a Foreign Member of the Swedish Royal Academy of Letters, History and Antiquities, and a Foreign Associate of the National Academy of Sciences of America. He has written several books and published many articles on Chinese archaeology in learned journals both in China and abroad.

AN ZHIMIN (安志敏) was born in 1924. He is Deputy Director and a research fellow of the Institute of Archaeology at the Chinese Academy of Social Sciences. He has directed several archaeological teams in the past thirty years. He specializes in the Neolithic Age archaeology of China. His interests also cover the archaeology of the Palaeolithic Age and the historical period. He has worked mainly in North China but also concurrently in the north-western and north-eastern parts. He has written several books and published over one hundred papers.

ZHANG CHANGSHOU (張長壽) was born in 1929. He graduated from the History Department of Yenching University in 1952. He is an associate research fellow of the Institute of Archaeology at the Chinese Academy of Social Sciences. He has long been engaged in field-work and specializes in archaeology of the Shang-Zhou period.

XU PINGFANG (徐苹芳) was born in 1930. He studied archaeology in the History Department of Beijing University and graduated in 1955. He has worked at the Institute of Archaeology at the Chinese Academy of Social Sciences since 1956. He is an associate research fellow. He specializes in archaeology of the Han-Tang period.

RECENT ARCHAEOLOGICAL DISCOVERIES IN THE PEOPLE'S REPUBLIC OF CHINA

THE INSTITUTE OF ARCHAEOLOGY
ACADEMY OF SOCIAL SCIENCES
PEOPLE'S REPUBLIC OF CHINA

The Centre for East Asian Cultural Studies

Unesco

First published 1984 by
The United Nations Educational, Scientific and Cultural Organization
7 Place de Fontenoy, 75700 Paris, France
and
The Centre for East Asian Cultural Studies
c/o The Toyo Bunko, Honkomagome 2-chome, 28–21
Bunkyo-ku, Tokyo, 113 Japan
Copyright © Unesco 1984

ISBN 4–89656–401–4 (CEACS)
ISBN 92–3–102241–5 (Unesco)

Printed in Japan by
Hinode Printing Co., Ltd.

Contents

List of Illustrations

PLATES

Preface

RECENT archaeological excavations in Asia have been motivated, on the one hand, by the growing interest of each nation in its own history, in an effort to know more about its past as well as about relations with neighbouring countries. On the other hand, everywhere there is an urgent need to conduct rescue or salvage excavations of specific sites that are threatened with destruction as the result of rapid urbanization and public and private construction works. In no period of Asian history has the demand for excavations been so great as it is now.

The current excavations in the region are being conducted by universities and museums as well as by governmental institutions. Their efforts have brought to light significant results. However, one of the difficulties faced by researchers is that the latest information on archaeological excavations and findings cannot be disseminated easily within the country concerned and much less exchanged with other countries owing to the lack of appropriate means at the national, regional, and international levels.

Furthermore, the results of the excavations should be disseminated amongst the general public also, since very little information is available about the ancient history and culture of Asian countries.

As a remedy to this, a new series of surveys on the archaeological sites and objects which have been excavated during the last twenty to thirty years and which are considered as having historical and cultural values were started by Unesco in 1979 as part of its programme on the study of Asian cultures, approved by the Twentieth Session of the General Conference held at Paris in October–November 1978.

This publication presents the results of the survey carried out by the Institute of Archaeology, Chinese Academy of Social Sciences, Beijing, People's Republic of China. The authors* are responsible for the choice and the presentation of the facts contained in this book and for the opinions expressed therein, which are not necessarily those of Unesco and do not engage the responsibility of the Organization.

---

* Text written by An Zhimin, Zhang Changshou, and Xu Pingfang, and edited by Xia Nai.

Recent Archaeological Discoveries in The People's Republic of China

CHINA is world-famous for its ancient civilization, long history, and splendid culture. Its rich cultural heritage provides an inexhaustible treasure-house for archaeological excavations and research.

China's archaeology goes back to ancient times. Epigraphy existed as long ago as the Northern Song dynasty (960–1127) and later developed into archaeology. In old China, archaeology rested on very weak foundations. Not until the beginning of the twentieth century did archaeology based on field excavations come into existence. Since the founding of the People's Republic of China in 1949, archaeological work has greatly developed. Archaeological investigations and excavations have been carried out throughout the country, from the Amur River (Heilongjiang) valley in the north-east to the Tibet (Xizang) Plateau in the south-west, from Xinjiang and the Mongolian prairies in the north-west to the Xisha Islands in the south-east. Our archaeological workers have ventured into every part of our country. Extensive efforts have been put into unearthing and studying the settlements of primitive society, the towns of feudal society, and burial places dating from various periods.

In short, over the past thirty years, China has made rich and outstanding archaeological discoveries. Owing to limitations of space, this book can deal only briefly with some of the most important ones, with a view to giving a general picture of China's archaeological work during that time.

1

1. The Traces of Ape-man

Dating from the Palaeolithic Age, traces of ape-man have been found throughout China. In addition to the fossil bones of *Dryopithecus* and *Ramapithecus* found in Yunnan Province and the teeth of *Australopithecus* found in Hubei Province, many fossils of *Homo erectus* have also been discovered. This shows that China is one of the important areas where studies of the origin of mankind should be pursued.

Yuanmou man (*Homo erectus yuanmouensis*) was found in Yunnan in 1965. The finds consisted of two front teeth and five pieces of stone implements including scrapers and choppers (fig. 1). According to palaeomagnetic dating, these finds date back some 1.7 million years. They are the most ancient human fossils and cultural relics ever discovered in China. But recent researches point to a later date, probably 500–600 thousand years, comparable to the date of the Lantian man mentioned next.

Lantian man (*Homo erectus lantianensis*), found in Shaanxi Province in 1963–64, is represented by his lower jaw-bone and skull. According to palaeomagnetic dating, the lower jaw-bone dates back 650 thousand years and the skull 750–800 thousand years. The stone implements found there, such as large choppers, scrapers, and pointed tools, are of a rather primitive character.

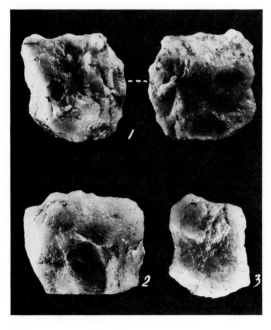

1 Stone implements of Yuanmou man unearthed in Yuanmou County, Yunnan

2　Sites at Zhoukoudian near Beijing

3　Skull fossils of Beijing man found at Zhoukoudian

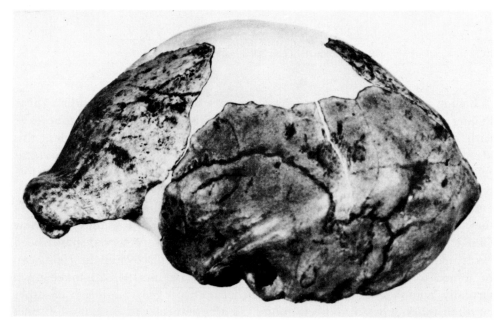

4   Stone implements of Beijing man found at Zhoukoudian

Beijing man (*Homo erectus pekinensis*) was found at Zhoukoudian near Beijing in 1929 (fig. 2).   The remains were discovered in a limestone cave with a stratigraphical deposit 40 metres deep.   For several decades, this place has been world-famous for the plentiful ape-man fossils and cultural relics which have been unearthed.   Before the liberation, altogether five skulls and other fossils representing more than forty individuals had been found.   These finds were of very high scientific value, but unfortunately they were lost during the Second World War.   Since the founding of New China, six teeth and one lower jaw-bone fairly well preserved have been excavated.   The frontal bone and occipital bone, discovered in 1966, can be joined to two pieces of broken skull discovered in 1943 to make up a virtually complete skull (fig. 3).   Furthermore, a great number of other cultural relics have also been found.   For instance, the existence of piles

4

of ashes in the cultural strata proves that Beijing man not only used fire but also knew how to manage it. The stone implements discovered have definite shapes, which shows that they served different purposes, and the fact that the stone implements in the upper strata are better made than those in the lower strata reflects the gradual development in tool manufacture (fig. 4). Using palaeomagnetic dating, it is estimated that the cave deposit, from the bottom to the top, was formed between 700 and 220 thousand years ago, which shows that men of the Beijing-man type lived there for a very, very long time.

Human fossils later than the ape-man were discovered in the following provinces: the Dali man in Shaanxi, Maba man in Guangdong, Changyang man in Hubei, and Dingcun man in Shanxi. Their physique had the features of Neanderthal man, indicating an advance in their evolution. As to their stone implements, they are more finely made and have an increasingly wider distribution than before.

2. *The Origin and Development of Microliths*

Men in the late Palaeolithic Age underwent great changes constitution-
ally and culturally. Upper Cave man found at Zhoukoudian and Liujiang
man found in Guangxi Province fall into the category of New Man. They
are the immediate ancestors of the present-day Chinese, showing some traits
common among the primitive Mongoloid peoples. Their stone implements
are more carefully made than before and their uses are more specifically
distinguished. In addition, the stone implements of north China made in
the late Palaeolithic Age tend to become smaller. With the increasing
use of hard small gravel as raw material, manufacturing techniques were
further improved, resulting in the specific technology of the manufacture
of microliths and exerting a wide influence on the later culture.

The earliest microliths are represented by the finds unearthed at Shiyu,
Shuo County, Shanxi Province, and those at Xiaonanhai, near the city of
Anyang, Henan Province (fig. 5). Despite the use of a rather primitive
chipping method, microliths in an embryonic form, such as small stones and
flakes, came into existence. According to Carbon-14 dating, the former go
back to as long ago as ca. 27000 B.C. and the latter to ca. 22000 B.C.

Typical microliths are represented by the finds unearthed at Xiachuan,
Qinshui County, Shanxi, and those at Hutouliang, Yangyuan County,
Hebei Province. They include various small core tools and long, thin
stone blades as well as finely made and varied scrapers and pointed tools.
According to Carbon-14 dating, the former date back to ca. 22000–14500 B.C.,
while the latter date from about nine thousand years ago. This fully con-
firms that typical microliths originated at the end of the late Palaeolithic
Age.

The remains of the Mesolithic Age found at Shayuan, Dali County,
Shaanxi (fig. 6), and those found at Lingjing, Xuchang County, Henan,
are also characterized by microliths. Since their strata belong to the Holo-
cene Age and they are not associated with potsherds, they are assumed to
be pre-ceramic remains of the Yellow River valley area. Later, with the
emergence and development of agriculture, microliths underwent a sudden
decline. Nevertheless, throughout the Neolithic Age, the Peiligang Culture,
Yangshao Culture, and Longshan Culture all continued to produce a small
quantity of microliths, and even as late as the Shang dynasty in the Bronze
Age there were still some left. These phenomena indicate that microliths
underwent a process of development and decline in the Yellow River valley.

Microliths are also widely distributed from the north-east via Inner

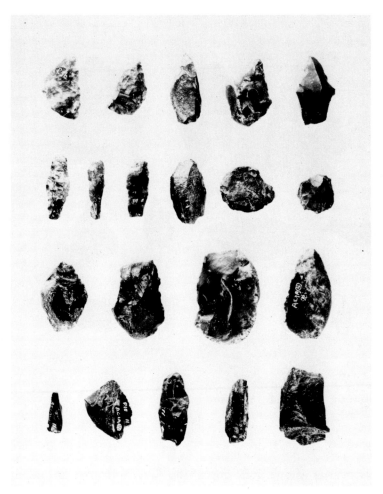

5 Microliths unearthed at Xiaonanhai, near the city of Anyang, Henan

Mongolia to the prairie of Xinjiang, and some of them even include different kinds of potsherds belonging to different ages and different cultural systems. Microlithic finds extended from the Mesolithic Age to the Neolithic Age, and a few to the twelfth and thirteenth centuries A.D.

In addition, in Tibet and Yunnan in the south-west, in Jiangsu Province along the lower reaches of the Yangtze River as well as in Guangdong Province in south China, microliths have also been found among the remains of different cultures and ages.

6   Microliths found at Shayuan, Dali County, Shaanxi

Archaeological discoveries show that microliths first appeared in north China and then spread widely within Chinese boundaries, and that they even extended to the vast areas in the north-east of Asia and the north-west of America. They reflected different cultures and lasted a long time. They nevertheless differ in shape from those found in Europe, North Africa, and West Asia. This is one of the archaeological questions of world significance which is worth exploring.

3. Discovery of Early Neolithic Remains

The missing links of the early Neolithic culture in the Yellow River valley were not filled in until the discovery of the ruins of Cishan in Wuan County, Hebei, and of Peiligang in Xinzheng County, Henan. Ruins of this kind have been found in more than forty places. The ruins of Cishan are scattered in the south of Hebei and the north of Henan whereas the ruins of Peiligang are located in the middle of Henan. Culturally speaking, they are similar in certain aspects but differ widely in others. There are still different opinions about whether they belong to the same culture.

The early Neolithic ruins show that the settlements were small and the cultural stratum thin. Nearly all the houses are round or square and semi-subterranean with narrow or tiered doorways. A number of storage pits lie nearby. Primitive kilns for pottery are found in some of the ruins. Clan graveyards usually lie in groups near the village. For instance, there are 114 tombs at Peiligang. They are crowded together in a regular pattern. Usually one man or woman is buried in one tomb; only in some tombs are two buried together. Pottery and stone vessels are found in the tombs. All this indicates that settled villages already existed at that time.

7 Stone quern and stone roller unearthed at Shuiquan, Jia County, Henan

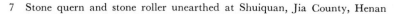

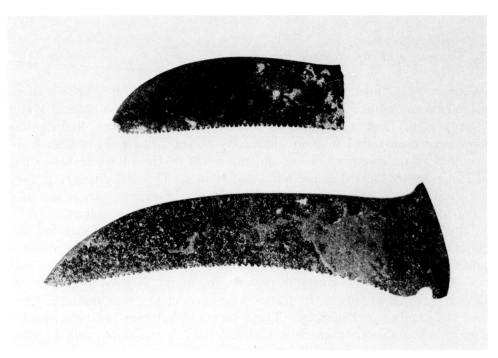

8 Stone sickles discovered at Ganghe, Changge County (*above*), and at Shuiquan, Jia County, Henan (*below*)

All the villages invariably bear the signs of an agricultural economy. The fine stone saddle-shaped quern with feet, the stone roller (fig. 7), the thin stone spade with a narrow and long curving edge, and the stone sickles with a saw-toothed edge (fig. 8) are all typical farming tools. The discovery of carbonized millet seeds there suggests that millet (*Sectaria italica*), a cultivated crop especially suitable to loess areas, has a very long history. In addition, the lifelike pottery sculpture in the shape of a pig's head and the large number of pig or dog skeletons are testimony of the existence of domestic animals. However, fishing, hunting, and gathering still played an important part. On the whole, economic life remained fairly primitive.

The pottery was handmade and its walls are of uneven thickness. The baking temperature was 700–930° C. Pottery objects are mainly of plain surface, red in colour, slightly polished, and sometimes decorated with a comb pattern. At Cishan, cord-marked pottery and even painted pottery has been found. Pottery is usually in the shape of round-bottomed bowls (*bo*), three-legged, round-bottomed bowls, two-eared, small-mouthed jars

10

9 Pottery jars unearthed at Peiligang, Xinzheng County (*left*), and at Shuiquan, Jia County, Henan (*right*)

(*hu*) (fig. 9), wide-mouthed jars (*guan*) with a deep body, and tripods (*ding*). Food containers (*yu*) and supporting feet for pottery vessels are only found at Cishan. The craft of pottery making, though primitive, laid a foundation for further development.

Stratigraphic analysis and Carbon-14 dating have proved that Peiligang dates from as long ago as 5500–4900 B.C. and Cishan from 5400–5100 B.C. They have an almost identical long history. They are obviously the forerunners of the Yangshao Culture and are at the root of many cultural elements of the Neolithic Age in the Yellow River valley, thus prolonging the continuity of cultural development in the Central Plains (the middle and lower reaches of the Yellow River). The remains of comb-pattern pottery found here are the earliest known. The remains of the same kind found in the north-east and in the coastal areas of the south-east must have some connection with those found in the north of China. These finds have played a significant role in the study of the origin and development of Neolithic culture in China.

4. *Distribution of the Yangshao Culture and Its Types*

The Yangshao Culture was discovered in Mianchi County, Henan, in 1921. Formerly the term "Painted-Pottery Culture" was employed to include the Yangshao Culture and many other types of cultures with painted pottery, which has caused great conceptual confusion. The work of the past thirty years has led to a more complete understanding of the Yangshao Culture. The Yangshao Culture, taking the Loess Plateau as a centre, spread along the middle reaches of the Yellow River. According to Carbon-14 dating, its date is about 4500–2500 B.C. and so it lasted more than two thousand years.

There exists some difference in cultural facies because of varying geographical distribution and age differences, and as a result, the culture is generally classified into various types which reflect these differences. For example, the sites on the Loess Plateau fall into the following four types: Beishouling, Banpo, Miaodigou, and Xiwangcun; the sites on the southeastern border of the Loess Plateau and North China Plains at the foot of the Taihang Mountains fall into the following types: Dahecun, Hougang, and Dasikongcun. The relative and absolute chronology of the different types has been determined by analysis of stratigraphic relations and cultural features as well as by Carbon-14 dating.

Life in settlements was fairly secure at that time. The sites vary in area from tens of thousands of square metres to one hundred thousand or more square metres. Excavation of Banpo in Xi'an and Jiangzhai in Lintong County, both in Shaanxi, has revealed the layout of the villages. At Jiangzhai, for example, the settlement is surrounded by a defensive moat and the houses are densely packed but in an orderly way. In the middle of the settlement is an open square around which the houses stand, their doors opening on to the square. There are five big houses, each of which has ten to twenty small- or medium-sized houses in its vicinity. There are three clan graveyards to the east of the moat. The tombs are arranged densely and in an orderly way with the heads of the dead facing west. Adults are buried in the tombs together with such burial objects as pottery and other articles for daily use. The funeral urns of children are buried around the houses. This discovery presents a vivid picture of human life at that time.

The houses were either semi-subterranean or surface buildings of wooden construction. Only their foundations remain in fairly good condition. Semi-subterranean houses were more popular and their square or rectangu-

12

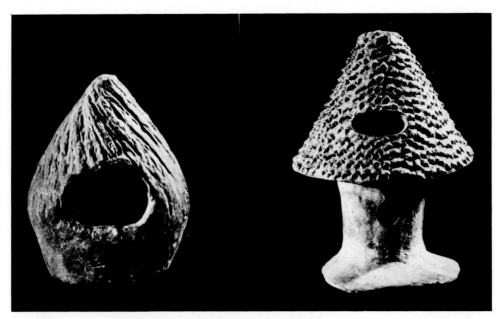

10 Pottery house models found at Youfeng, Wugong County, Shaanxi

lar foundations generally have an area of about 20 square metres. The area of the remains of the largest one found at Banpo is more than 100 square metres; this must have been a public place where members of a clan used to gather. Surface houses are either round or rectangular. The pottery house model found at Youfeng, Wugong County, Shaanxi, shows that the roof of a round house was cone-shaped (fig. 10). The rectangular house found at Dahecun, Zhengzhou, Henan, has three rooms linked together and a partition in the biggest room, thus constituting a complete building with an area of over 70 square metres (fig. 11). All this proves that the house-building technique of the Yangshao Culture reached a high level.

Agricultural economy was well developed. In addition to millet growing, vegetables were planted. There were simple farming tools such as stone spades for digging and stone and pottery sickles for harvesting. The stone saddle-shaped querns which had prevailed before gradually disappeared. Domestic animals were mainly pigs and dogs, and it has not yet been proved whether other species were tamed.

Differences in age and regional variations resulted in a disparity in the shape, type, and design of pottery vessels. Common pottery vessels include flat-bottomed or ring-footed bowls (*wan*), round-bottomed bowls, tubs (*pen*),

11   Ruins of house foundations of the Yangshao Culture at Dahecun, Zhengzhou, Henan

wide-mouthed jars, tripods, and small-mouthed, pointed-bottomed bottles (*ping*) (fig. 12).   So far as patterns are concerned, besides cord marks, red and black designs painted on polished pottery are most noteworthy.   Some pottery is coated with white slip before being painted.   Painted pottery varies in quantity and in design with the passage of time.   On the Loess Plateau, for example, in the Beishouling type of the early period, painted pottery was rare except for some round-bottomed bowls with painted rims. In the Banpo type, painted pottery increased in quantity and was often decorated with different triangular motifs (pl. 1) as well as with lifelike human faces and animal motifs representing fish, birds, and frogs.   In the Miaodigou type, painted pottery was more popular, with such motifs as round dots, triangular whorls, and arcs, distinctive by reason of their rich colours (pl. 2).   Some vessels have animal motifs of frogs and birds, and some are coated with white slip or painted in both red and black, thus adding to their artistic quality.   In the Xiwangcun type of the late period, painted pottery was on the decline both in quantity and as regards pattern. This change reflects the basic rule of elaboration or simplification of the patterns in the development of the painted pottery of the Yangshao Culture.

14

12 Small-mouthed, pointed-
    bottomed pottery bottle
    unearthed at Jiangzhai,
    Lintong County, Shaanxi

The development of the Yangshao Culture in the Central Plains, which began early and lasted long, served as a link to the next culture and exerted a tremendous influence on nearby regions. For example, the painted pottery of the Majiayao Culture in the upper reaches of the Yellow River, of the Dawenkou Culture in the lower reaches, of the Hongshan Culture in the north-east of China, and of both the Daxi Culture and the Qujialing Culture in the middle reaches of the Yangtze River were all related to that of the Yangshao Culture. All this shows the important role of the Yangshao Culture in the history of cultural development in China.

15

5. Cemeteries of the Dawenkou Culture

The Dawenkou Culture was discovered in Taian County, Shandong Province, in 1959. Of over one hundred sites already located, more than ten have been excavated. Most of them have groups of tombs, numbering about fifteen hundred, and a great variety of grave-goods. Though available information about the houses and storage pits of the culture is still fragmentary, it can be inferred that its agricultural economy reached a fairly high level. The Dawenkou Culture is chiefly distributed around the lower reaches of the Yellow River. As for the Qingliangang Culture found in the north of Jiangsu, some scholars consider it as belonging to the early period of the Dawenkou Culture while others regard it as another culture which appeared earlier than the Dawenkou Culture. However, most scholars hold that both are part of the same culture.

The cemeteries of the Dawenkou Culture often present the phenomenon of superimposition and the intrusion of tombs. For the most part, one person is buried in one tomb. There are a few tombs in which a man and a woman are buried together, with the former on the left and the latter on the right. In some others, children are buried together with

13 Multiple burial tomb found at Dawenkou, Taian County, Shandong

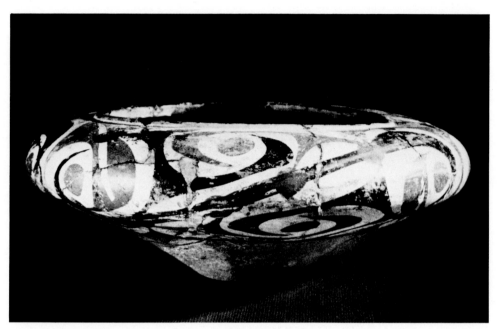

14 Painted pottery basin unearthed at Dadunzi, Pi County, Jiangsu

adults (fig. 13). Tombs vary in size and in the quantity of grave-goods—possibly a sign of disparity between rich and poor. In a big tomb there would be a wooden burial chamber and more than one hundred funeral objects including a large number of pottery, stone and bone articles, and fine jade and ivory objects. Even pigs' heads were used as burial objects, and in some cases more than ten pigs' heads have been found in one tomb. Generally speaking, there is no coffin in a small tomb, and only a few simple grave-goods, and in some cases no such ones are found at all. Skeletons are often found with deformed skulls and front teeth extracted, which was perhaps a common practice at that time. However, they bear a physical resemblance to those of the Yangshao Culture.

The plentiful grave-goods show that handicrafts were well developed at that time. Pottery of the early period was largely red and handmade, and was supplanted in the late period by grey pottery made by the true potter's wheel. In addition, there was also fine black pottery, white pottery, and thin "eggshell pottery." The pottery found mainly has a plain surface, but there are also examples of painted pottery, openwork pottery, or incised-patterned pottery. Painted pottery is mostly coated with red or white slip, then painted in black or red with geometrical motifs. Some vessels are similar to those of the Yangshao Culture (fig. 14). Pottery is made in many different

17

15 Animal-shaped pottery pitcher unearthed at Dawenkou, Taian County, Shandong

shapes: tripods, wide-mouthed jars, small-mouthed jars, pitchers (*gui*), covered, spouted, loop-handled, three-legged wine vessels (*he*), beakers (*gu*), stemmed bowls (*dou*), and hanging bottles (*beihu*) are representative examples. Some pitchers are even made in the shape of animals (fig. 15), which is a unique style. Stone implements are mostly polished and made with extra care. An advanced technique of drilling was applied in making holes. Stone implements include such working tools as axes, adzes, and chisels. Elegantly shaped jade spades have been found (pl. 3), and there are quite a number of exquisite ornaments, for example, jade rings and pendants, a sixteen-toothed ivory comb in openwork, an ivory tube with a four-petal design in openwork, and a carved bone tube ingeniously studded with turquoise bead inlay. These works of art are an embodiment of wisdom and creativity of our forefathers and display a development of technology which is unique in its brilliance.

18

According to Carbon-14 dating, the Dawenkou Culture goes back to 3400–2200 B.C. and lasted more than two thousand years, corresponding to the middle and the late periods of the Yangshao Culture. The Dawenkou Culture had its own distribution and its unique cultural features. It was on the basis of the Dawenkou Culture that the Shandong Longshan Culture developed. The relationships which arose from such a close succession are especially apparent in the craft of pottery making.

6. *The Origin and Development of the Longshan Culture*

The Longshan Culture discovered in Zhangqiu County, Shandong, in 1928 contains relics from the late Neolithic Age. Thanks to extensive research, it has come to be better known. This culture was a development of the Yangshao Culture, had a wider geographical distribution, spreading almost all over the Yellow River valley, and had outstanding regional features. It is therefore clearly wrong to believe that the Longshan Culture had one single origin or that the culture spread from east to west, as was believed in the past. For the sake of convenience, the Longshan Culture is usually preceded by the name of a province or given the name of a culture as a means of distinction: for instance, the Shandong Longshan Culture (typical Longshan Culture), Henan Longshan Culture (Hougong II Culture), Shaanxi Longshan Culture (Keshengzhuang II Culture), and Zhejiang Longshan Culture (Liangzhu Culture). The scope of the Longshan Culture may be further enlarged to include the Qijia Culture at the upper reaches of the Yellow River. What is more important is the Miaodigou II Culture which belongs to the early Longshan Culture. It assimilated some elements of the Yangshao Culture and was the forerunner of the Henan Longshan Culture. As for the Shandong Longshan Culture, it derived from the Dawenkou Culture. Therefore, by the Longshan Culture we actually mean cultural heritages which had different origins and interacted with one another. Nevertheless, their common cultural features were stronger than their own separate characteristics.

The settlements of the Longshan Culture are generally more extensive than those of the Yangshao Culture, but their layout is not yet very clear. If we consider the Baiying site in Tangyin County, Henan, for instance, within a space of 1,000 square metres stand forty-six houses, mainly in rows from east to west and in lines from north to south. Building foundations are superimposed layer upon layer. The increasing deposit has made the whole site a raised platform. The houses underwent a process of transformation from semi-subterranean to surface. Most of them are round buildings surrounded by walls made out of clay mixed with straw or adobe. The floor inside the house is rammed and covered by a thin layer of lime to prevent dampness from entering. The fact that people began to use lime as building material is a phenomenon worthy of note. Not many graveyards have been found here, apart from some clan graves around the settlement containing a few grave-goods. The practice of burying funeral urns for children within the foundation walls of the buildings or somewhere near the houses differs slightly from that of the Yangshao Culture.

16 Red pottery pitcher unearthed in Weifang County, Shandong

17 (*left*) Black pottery casket and (*right*) covered jar unearthed at Sanlihe, Jiao County, Shandong

The agricultural economy was fairly well developed at that time. Millet remained the main crop, but the types of farm tools increased. In addition to stone shovels and knives, there were two-toothed wooden digging tools (*lei*), stone sickles, shell sickles, etc. The variety of domestic animals had also increased: dogs, pigs, cattle, sheep, goats, and chickens were raised.

Grey pottery was the main potteryware for daily use (except in the Qijia Culture). Pottery of different colours such as grey, black, and red was produced as a result of proper control of the atmosphere inside the kiln. Some white pottery was also made with kaolin clay. Compared with

22

18 Cord-marked pottery jars unearthed at Huogang, Anyang County, Henan

the pottery of the Yangshao Culture, big changes in shape and design are to be noted. For instance, round-mouthed, three-legged wine vessels (*jia*), cooking tripods with hollow legs (*li*), steamers with three hollow feet (*yan*), pitchers (fig. 16), *he* wine vessels, stemmed bowls, basins, and cups (*bei*), all have new shapes. The surface is mostly polished (fig. 17). In some areas, cord marks (fig. 18), basket marks, and check patterns are used in varying degrees as decorations. Fragments of painted pottery of the early Longshan Culture have been found. During the late period in particular, a potter's wheel was widely used and the pottery became so thin that eggshell pottery of 1–2 millimetres in thickness emerged, which symbolizes a new high point in the craft of pottery making.

According to Carbon-14 dating, the Longshan Culture lasted about five hundred years, from 2300 to 1800 B.C. Nevertheless, some of its remains, such as those of the Shandong Longshan Culture and Qijia Culture, have an even longer history—their lower limit may be as late as 1500 B.C. The Longshan Culture in the Central Plains inherited the Yangshao Culture and then developed, and on its basis arose the Erlitou Culture of the early Shang dynasty. It is clear that they developed in close relation from the same origin and it is therefore beyond doubt that the Longshan Culture was a forerunner of China's ancient civilization and that it was related to the succeeding Shang and Zhou cultures.

23

7. *The Hemudu Culture: Remains of an Ancient Culture Which Practised Rice Cultivation*

The Hemudu ruins were found in Yuyao County, Zhejiang Province, in 1973. An area of 2,600 square metres has been excavated and a large number of remains of wooden buildings and rich cultural relics have been unearthed. The Hemudu ruins are one of the earlier sites in the lower reaches of the Yangtze River. Sites of similar culture are believed to be widespread in the Hangzhou Gulf and its vicinity.

The remains of the wooden buildings discovered here consist, for the most part, of wooden piles driven row upon row into the subsoil, scattered beams and pillars, and 0.8–1 metre long planks (fig. 19). What a pity these structures can no longer be restored! Several scores of wooden structural members with mortise and tenon joints have also been found here. For instance, small tenons have been chiselled at both ends of wooden pillars,

19 Remains of the wooden buildings found at Hemudu, Yuyao County, Zhejiang

24

20 Bone digging tools unearthed at Hemudu

and some of the pillars have been holed to receive the tenons. This reveals that the craft of wood construction had reached a fairly high level artistically and technically. The sites of "pile-dwelling" buildings and pottery house models have often been discovered among the remains in the middle and the lower reaches of the Yangtze River and in areas of south China, representing the architectural style of the humid zones. Judging from the remains and constructions, they probably belong to the same category, yet this question calls for further study.

It is worth noting that among the remains a large quantity of rice has been discovered, some of which is mixed with husks, stalks, and leaves. These remains mark the ancient sites where long-grained non-glutinous rice (*Oryza sativa indica*, subspecies of *hsien ting*) was cultivated. It probably shows that the lower reaches of the Yangtze River were one of the important regions where paddy rice originated. Other evidence of the development of agriculture is the existence of the bone digging tools made of buffaloes' shoulder-blades. They have sharp edges, shallow grooves, and holes and can be fixed on to a wooden handle to facilitate digging (fig. 20). The discovery of a large number of wild animals, fish, and shellfish, in addition to domestic animals such as pigs and dogs, indicates that fishing, hunting, and gathering played a fairly important place in the economic life of the people.

25

21 (*left*) Pottery basin and (*right*) jar unearthed at Hemudu

Handicrafts were quite a flourishing industry. Finely made wooden articles such as shovels, spears, mallets, pestles, oars, and tool-handles as well as bone objects such as digging tools (*si*), arrow heads, needles, awls, daggers, dartlike spears for fishing, and decorative articles were made with polished stone axes and chisels. On some bone and ivory objects, lively designs of birds were even engraved. All these represent a very high level of craftsmanship.

Nevertheless, the technical level of pottery making seems to be rather primitive. Most of the pottery is handmade black charcoal pottery, the clay being mixed with carbonized plant stalks, leaves, and rice husks. Such pottery is porous and thick, irregular in shape, and has a low baking temperature (approximately 850°C). Its polished surface is often decorated with cord marks and incised patterns or with lively animal and plant motifs. In addition, three pieces of painted pottery have been discovered which may have some connection with the Yangshao Culture. Most of the vessels are kettles or cauldrons (*fu*) and wide-mouthed jars (fig. 21). There are also tubs, basins, stemmed bowls, vessel covers, and vessel-supporting feet, of which kettles or cauldrons and vessel-supporting feet are the most representative.

The Hemudu Culture, as indicated by Carbon-14 dating, lasted from 4400 to 3300 B.C., representing the earlier Neolithic remains of this area. The Majiabang and Liangzhu Cultures developed from the Hemudu Culture but are more extensively dispersed and have more things in common with the Longshan Culture. This shows the incessant interplay and mutual influence of the Neolithic cultures in the Yangtze and Yellow river valleys.

8. The Early Period of Development in South China

The early Neolithic culture in south China can be roughly divided into two periods—the early and the late.

The early Neolithic culture, characterized by crude pottery with cord marks, was widely scattered in Jiangxi, Guangxi, Guangdong, Fujian, and Taiwan Provinces, and therefore symbolizes different types of culture. It went through a long period of development. These cultures have something in common with one another. For instance, there are large numbers of chipped stone implements as well as polished ones, and the pottery objects commonly used are primitive, simple, and crude, requiring a low baking temperature, in some cases only 680° C. Fishing, hunting, and gathering held the central place in economic life, while the development of agriculture was not yet noticeable and animal husbandry not flourishing, thus reflecting the economic backwardness of the society. The late emergence of agriculture in this area and the cord marks and comb patterns on the earthenware similar to those in the Central Plains are further indications that the Neolithic culture in south China had a close connection with the culture in north China. Very often there is a big margin of error in Carbon-14 dating for the specimens found in the south China limestone area, usually causing dates to be attributed to an earlier period. Different substances from the same stratum may be separated by a margin of several thousand years. Therefore, the age of the early remains in this area is still an outstanding issue. It is estimated, however, that the upper age limit of the remains may be not earlier than 4000–5000 B.C.

During the late Neolithic culture period, there was a remarkable development in pottery with more variety in both quality and colour, and there appeared a kind of hard pottery with a kiln temperature as high as 1,100° C. The vessels, mostly kettles or cauldrons, tripods, pitchers, food containers (*guǐ*), stemmed bowls, small-mouthed jars, and small cups, were shaped by hand and then perfected on a slow-turning potter's wheel. The majority of them have a plain surface. Most of the decorated ware has cord marks, but a few are either geometrically impressed or printed. Stone implements are quite finely polished and much varied, there being adzes with holes, stepped or shouldered adzes, etc. The discovery of rice at some of the sites shows that agriculture had considerably developed. There are not many house ruins found, but pottery house models in the form of pile-dwelling, discovered at Yingpanli, Qingjiang County, Jiangxi, have provided valuable material for reconstructing the architecture of the time (fig. 22). The "longer-ridged but shorter-eaved" primitive roof structure is worth noting.

22 Pottery house models discovered at Yingpanli, Qingjiang County, Jiangxi

It was very popular in ancient Asia and there probably existed certain cultural exchanges and mutual influences.

Owing to age and area differences, the cultures have different facies as well as different Carbon-14 dates. For instance, the Shanbie Culture of Xiushui County, Jiangxi Province, dates back to 2335 ± 95 B.C.; the Shixia Culture of Qujiang, Guangdong, dates back to 2070 ± 100 B.C.; the Tanshishan Culture (middle stratum) of Minhou, Fujian, dates back to 1140 ± 90 B.C.; and the Fengbitou Culture of Gaoxiong, Taiwan, dates back to 2050 ± 200 B.C. Although there is quite a disparity in age between the Tanshishan Culture and the Fengbitou Culture, they resemble each other fairly closely, especially as regards painted pottery, and hence they should belong to the same cultural system. From this we can see that as far back as 1000–2000 B.C. the inhabitants of ancient China were already crossing the Taiwan Strait.

In south China, the different kinds of the late Neolithic culture have many things in common. They are very similar to the Qujialing Culture in the Jianghan area, and at the same time they include some elements of the Longshan Culture. This fully reflects the fact that in the late Neolithic Age in China the Neolithic cultures of different origins were tending towards gradual unification. In addition, hard pottery with geometric designs began to develop, and thus were laid the foundations for its spread in the Shang and Zhou dynasties. This type of ware not only showed exceptional ingenuity in the craft of pottery making but also heralded the invention of proto-porcelain.

29

9. The Erlitou Culture

The first dynasty in China's history is the Xia dynasty (21st–16th century B.C.). Archaeologists, however, differ in their views on what constitutes the remains of the Xia culture. Some hold that the Erlitou Culture is the same thing as the Xia culture, while others believe that the Erlitou Culture belongs to the early Shang dynasty, whereas only the earlier Longshan Culture in Henan should fall into the category of the Xia culture. This will probably remain a disputed issue for many years to come, so we will leave it for the time being. Let us first take a look at the main contents and characteristics of this type of culture.

The Erlitou Culture was discovered in Yanshi County, Henan, in the mid-1950s. Its remains are mainly distributed in the west of Henan and the south of Shanxi. Up to now more than ten sites have been excavated, among which the Erlitou site is the most important and one of the earliest discovered, which is why the culture has been called the Erlitou Culture.

One of the most important discoveries among the Erlitou remains is the site of a large palace. The base of Palace Building 1 is a rammed-earth

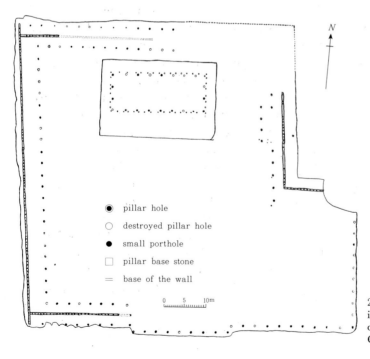

23 Plan of Palace Build-
ing 1 of the early Shang
dynasty at Erlitou, Yanshi
County, Henan

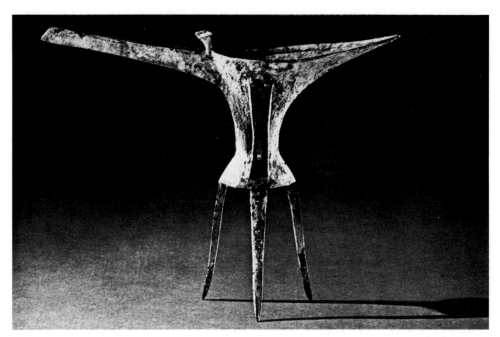

24 Bronze *jue* wine vessel unearthed at Erlitou

platform measuring 108 metres from east to west and 100 metres from north to south. On this base, to the north of centre, is a rectangular hall foundation in which pillar holes are evenly located. Presumably it was a building with a floor space of 30.4 metres on its long side (with nine pillars) and 11.4 metres on its short side (with four pillars), having a hipped roof extending over the eaves. The whole base is surrounded by walls. The evenly spaced pillar holes inside or on both sides of the walls suggest that there might have been some corridors and side-rooms (fig. 23). The front doorway is in the middle of the southern part of the base. This is also about 30 metres wide with nine pillars, which shows how magnificent the building must have been.

The discovery of this large palace indicates that the place is probably the site of a capital. According to historical documents, Xibo, the capital of the first emperor of the Shang dynasty, was situated somewhere in this county. A recently discovered walled city with an enclosure wall about 1.2 × 1.7 kilometres in length is probably the site of Xibo. It is situated about 5–6 kilometres north-east of Erlitou and dated in the last phase of the Erlitou Culture or possibly a little later. Ruins of several palaces and other buildings have been found inside the city wall. It was discovered in 1983, and its excavation started in the spring of 1984.

31

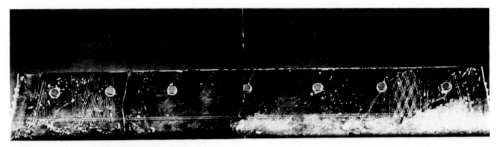

25 Jade knife unearthed at Erlitou

Another important discovery at Erlitou was that of the earliest bronze containers ever known. Since 1973 four or five loop-handled, three-legged bronze wine vessels of *jue* type have been unearthed there. The best one has a long spout, three long legs, and a handle at one side. It measures 22.5 centimetres in height with a small waist and a flat bottom (fig. 24). Although the bronze containers dug up at the Erlitou site are small in number, lack variety and are mostly simple in design, yet they required quite complicated moulds and techniques and thus by no means belong to the initial stage of bronze casting. The art of inlaying was also well developed. For instance, a piece of bronze round plaque unearthed from the Erlitou site measures 17 centimetres in diameter and 0.5 centimetre in thickness. It is inlaid with sixty-one pieces of rectangular turquoise at its rim like the graduations on watches or clocks and has two rows of cross-shaped turquoise inlays across its body, thirteen in each row. It provides a good insight into the superb craftsmanship of inlaying of that time.

Jades were also discovered in the Erlitou remains, such as a semi-transparent jade knife, 65 centimetres long, with rhombic designs engraved on both ends (fig. 25). In addition, there is a jade ornament like a square rod in shape, measuring 17.1 centimetres in length. It is divided into six parts, alternately carved with strings, petal motifs, or animal faces, displaying a high level of jade-carving craftsmanship.

The Erlitou Culture pottery had its own distinctive features and is found in a variety of shapes such as tripods, wine vessels of *he, jia, jiao,* and *jue* types, and beakers; some of them are decorated all over with parallel rows of applied decoration, while others are engraved with fish designs, dragon-like animal (*kui*) designs, or twin-dragon motifs, and others still with various kinds of symbols.

The Erlitou Culture is obviously different from the Longshan Culture of the last phase of primitive society. Magnificent palace buildings and the emergence of bronze objects mark the beginning of a new era.

32

10. The Early Cities of the Shang Dynasty

Shangcheng in the city of Zhengzhou is the site of the capital of the Shang dynasty (16th–11th century B.C.) and antedates the Anyang ruins of the Yin (the later period of the Shang) dynasty. It was discovered in the early 1950s. The Shang culture remains in Zhengzhou, represented by Erligang, are concentrated in the site of Shangcheng.

Shangcheng had been the earliest site of a walled city until an earlier Shang city site (probably Xibo) was discovered in Yanshi County in 1983. It is surrounded by a wall of rammed earth which excavations have shown to measure about 7 kilometres in length (fig. 26). The fact that the present city of Zhengzhou was built directly on top of Shangcheng has caused a good deal of inconvenience in archaeological excavation. However, in the excavated north-east part of the city, remains of many large rammed-earth foundations have been discovered, indicating that there was once a large architectural complex there.

26   Shang sites in Zhengzhou

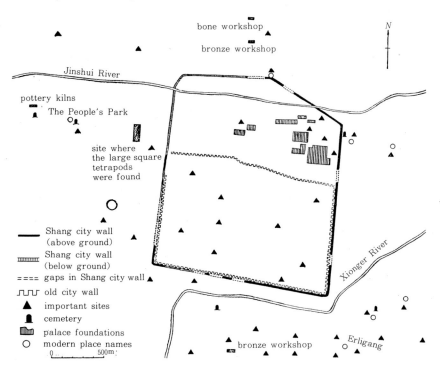

33

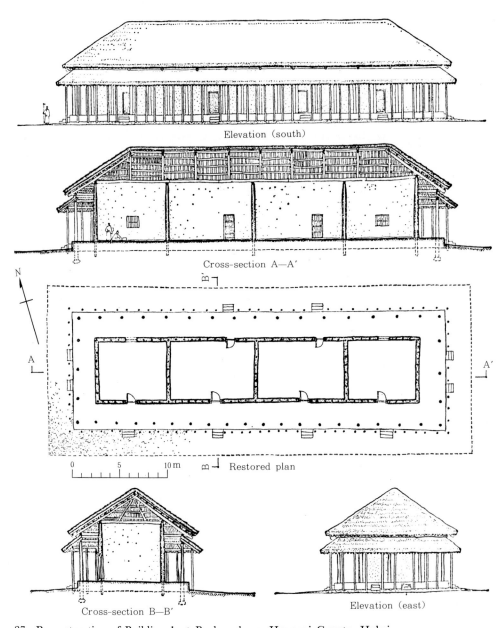

Elevation (south)

Cross-section A—A′

Restored plan

0   5   10 m

Cross-section B—B′

Elevation (east)

27   Reconstruction of Building 1 at Panlongcheng, Huangpi County, Hubei

34

The discovery of residential ruins and the remains of the Shang dynasty workshops for bronze casting, pottery making, and bone engraving in the periphery of Shangcheng have given some idea of the layout inside and outside the city. Tombs with bronze vessels have also been found at Peijiachuan, Mingoulu, and other places. Especially important is the discovery of two large bronze tetrapods (*fangding*) unearthed on the western outskirts of the city, measuring respectively 100 and 87 centimetres in height. Both of them are square with raised designs of a legendary animal *taotie* and bosses on the four sides (pl. 4). They indicate the tremendous development that had taken place in bronze casting.

Another city of the Shang dynasty is Panlongcheng in Huangpi County, Hubei. It is as ancient as Shangcheng but is smaller in scale, measuring only 1 kilometre or so in circumference with a 10-metre-wide moat outside the city wall. There is a large rammed-earth platform base in the northeast of the city, upon which the remains of three buildings have been found side by side. The unearthed base of Building 1 is 39.8 metres in length from east to west, and 12.3 metres in width from north to south. It can be inferred from the layout of the pillars and other traces that there might have been a palace structure with four big rooms in the centre, surrounded by verandahs. It had a roof supported by four beams, with eaves one on top of another, and brick-surfaced aprons around the structure to protect the foundations from rain (fig. 27).

Outside Panlongcheng there are tombs of the same period with rich stores of grave-goods. Tombs 1 and 2 at Lijiazui in the eastern suburbs of the ruined city are the most important. Both are rectangular pit tombs without passageways, but they have carved wooden coffins and a large quantity of grave-goods. Each tomb has a group of bronze ceremonial vessels, such as tripods, cooking tripods with hollow legs, steamers with three hollow legs, food containers, beakers, wine vessels of *jue*, *jia*, *he*, urn-shaped *lei*, and swing-handled *you* types (fig. 28), and basins—most of them with raised or sunken *taotie* designs as well as circlets, whorl motifs, etc. The biggest object unearthed there is a bronze tripod, measuring 55 centimetres in height, which is only second in size to the above-mentioned two large tetrapods of the same period found in Zhengzhou.

In addition, a large bronze axelike weapon (*yue*), 41 centimetres long, with a dragonlike animal motif, and a 50-centimetre-long jade dagger-axe (*ge*) have been found among the grave-goods, probably symbolizing the power and influence of the dead.

There are striking resemblances in many respects between the remains found at Shangcheng in Zhengzhou and those found at Panlongcheng, though the former are located in the Yellow River valley in the north of China and the latter in the Yangtze River valley in the south of China.

28　Bronze *you* wine vessel unearthed at Panlongcheng

The discovery has dissipated the traditional idea that the culture of the Yin dynasty only spread out in the Yellow River valley and has therefore expanded the sphere of study of the Yin culture.

11. An Unprecedented Discovery among the Yin Ruins: Fu Hao's Tomb

The famous Anyang ruins of the Yin dynasty mark the site of the capital of the late Shang dynasty. Scientific excavations began as early as 1928, bringing to light a large quantity of precious and valuable remains such as the palace ruins at Xiaotuncun and the Xibeigang royal cemetery in the village of Houchiazhuang as well as bronze vessels, jade objects, stone sculptures, bone engravings, and oracle bones with inscriptions. However, work was suspended in 1937 owing to the outbreak of the war between China and Japan (1937–45).

As soon as the Institute of Archaeology of the Chinese Academy of Sciences was founded in 1950, the excavation was immediately resumed. In the spring of 1950, a tomb at Wuguancun was excavated. It is one of the large tombs in the eastern area of Xibeigang. Although its chamber had been robbed, the immolated persons and grave-goods on both sides of the two-tiered platform were fairly well preserved. On the west side of the platform, a stone chime (*qing*) measuring 84 centimetres in length with a tiger design was found. It is an exceptionally exquisite musical instrument of the Yin dynasty (fig. 29).

29 Stone chime unearthed at the big tomb at Wuguancun, Anyang, Henan

30 Animal-shaped bronze wine vessel unearthed from Fu Hao's tomb in Anyang

To the south-west of the Wuguan tomb is a vast stretch of sacrificial pits, of which more than one thousand were unearthed in 1934–35, and to the east over one hundred and eighty were excavated in 1976. They are all rectangular pits arranged in good order, and in each of them are buried either the beheaded trunks or heads only of eight to ten persons. That human beings were used as sacrifices on such a large scale is a most convincing indication of the nature of the society of the Yin dynasty.

However, in the excavations of the ruins of the Yin dynasty in recent years, no discovery was more surprising than that of the tomb of Fu Hao, King Wu Ding's spouse, near Xiaotuncun in 1976. This is the first intact tomb of a member of the royal family of the Shang dynasty unearthed so far. It is not large, neither has it any passageways, yet it is exceptionally rich in grave-goods—more than two hundred bronze ceremonial vessels (fig. 30) and over seven hundred pieces of jade, in addition to stone implements, ivory carvings (pl. 5), and so forth. Most of the bronze vessels bear inscriptions, the majority of them being to the memory of Fu Hao. Among the bronze vessels, there is a rectangular twin wine vessel (*fangyi*) shaped

31　Rectangular bronze twin wine vessel unearthed from Fu Hao's tomb in Anyang

like two square vessels linked together. It measures 60 centimetres in height with a lid resembling a hipped roof (fig. 31). There is also a 44.5-centimetre-high triplex *yan* steamer, similar to a rectangular table with six legs, in which there are three round holes each holding a steamer (*zeng*). The shape of these two bronzeware is unique, and the like of them have never been seen before.

The jade objects from Fu Hao's tomb are also very exquisite. There are more than ten figurines (fig. 32), round or relief sculptures of human figures in immaculate dress, as well as a naked half-feminine–half-masculine figure (pl. 6). In addition, there are over 160 animal carvings, including realistic or imaginary birds and beasts in round sculpture or in relief. All the objects, without exception, are lifelike and ingeniously carved. In a word, the discovery of Fu Hao's tomb is unprecedented in the history of excavation at Anyang, and it is no exaggeration to call it a treasure-house of the Yin dynasty.

The Yin ruins at Anyang was first famous for its inscriptions on oracle bones. Since the excavation of a large quantity of oracle bones at Pit 127 in

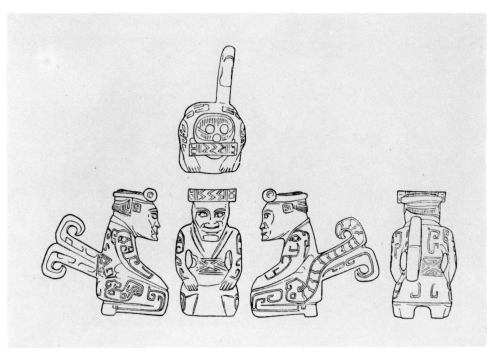

32 Jade figurine unearthed from Fu Hao's tomb in Anyang

1936, very few have been dug up by scientific excavation. It was not until recently that any new discoveries were made. In 1973 over forty-seven hundred fragments of inscribed oracle bones were brought to light in the south of Xiaotuncun. It was the largest number of oracle bones unearthed in recent years. According to the location of the excavation and the content of the inscriptions, most of them were considered to belong to the Wu Yi period (ca. 1130–1095 B.C.) (fig. 33). Apart from the ruins at Anyang, other important discoveries in the late Shang dynasty remains have been made in the following places: Gaocheng County, Hebei Province; Pinggu, Beijing; Yidu, Shandong; Shilou, Shanxi; Ningxiang, Hunan; and Qingjiang, Jiangxi.

The iron blade of an axe with a bronze handle found at Taixicun in Gaocheng has been identified as being made of meteoric iron (pl. 7). Also another bronze axe with an iron blade has been unearthed at Liujiahe in Pinggu County and its blade been found to be made of meteoric iron, too. Considering the two bronze weapons with meteoric iron blades from the early Western Zhou dynasty (11th century–771 B.C.) which were unearthed in Xun County, Henan, early in 1931, the new discoveries at Taixicun and Liujiahe have led to dating the use of meteoric iron in ancient China to two or three hundred years earlier than had previously been thought.

33   Inscribed oracle bones unearthed at Xiaotuncun, Anyang

In the south of China, bronzes from the late Yin dynasty have been discovered in many places in Hunan, especially in Ningxiang County. They are all finely crafted and beautiful. A kind of big bells made of bronze (*nao*) are the most noteworthy.   The Wucheng ruins in Qingjiang are the Yin ruins in south China where fairly large-scale excavations have been carried out.   Discoveries include houses, pottery kilns, tombs, and other remains as well as symbols and inscriptions engraved on earthenware which provide important material for the study of relations between the northern and southern regions of the Yin culture.

12. New Discoveries at Zhouyuan

To the north of Qishan and Fufeng Counties, Shaanxi, lies a high mountain called Qishan, at the southern foot of which is a stretch of plain, namely, Zhouyuan. It was the early capital of the Zhou dynasty before it conquered the Yin dynasty. Afterwards, the capital was moved to Feng and Hao during the reigns of King Wen (ca. 1088–1038 B.C.) and King Wu (ca. 1038–1025 B.C.); yet Zhouyuan still remained one of the important political centres in the Western Zhou dynasty.

Zhouyuan was known in the past for the continuous discoveries there of bronze vessels of the Western Zhou dynasty. However, not until 1976 when a large-scale excavation was undertaken and big building sites and inscribed oracle bones of the Western Zhou dynasty were found, did a breakthrough come about in archaeological work at Zhouyuan.

The excavation in 1976 at Fengchucun in Qishan County revealed the foundations of a building complex. The whole building stands on a rammed-earth base which measures 45.2 metres long from north to south by 32.5 metres wide from east to west. The layout of the building, taking the doorway and the front hall as its axis, provides wing-rooms on either side, forming a compound in which are two rows of houses and a symmetrical arrangement of rooms (fig. 34). The front hall was the main part of the building, situated in the centre of the compound, with a floor space measuring 17.2 metres from east to west with seven rows of pillar holes and 6.1 metres from north to south with four rows of pillar holes. The front hall had a courtyard to its south and was surrounded by verandahs which linked it with the wing-rooms on either side and with the yard to the rear. In addition, drainage facilities have been discovered in both courtyards. The discovery of a large quantity of scorched red earth covering the foundations and the late Western Zhou dynasty remains leads to the assumption that the buildings were burnt down during the late Western Zhou dynasty.

The sites of large buildings as well as a great number of wide-curved roof tiles, semi-circular roof tiles, and eave tiles have been discovered in Shaochencun in Fufeng County. The tiling of roofs probably started in the Western Zhou dynasty. Buildings with tiled roofs were no ordinary dwelling houses: they might have been palaces, temples, and the like.

In a wing-room on the western side of the above-mentioned large building at Fengchucun, a storage pit has been discovered from which more than seventeen thousand fragments of tortoise-shell have been retrieved. Of these, over 190 are incised with inscriptions including divinations for offering

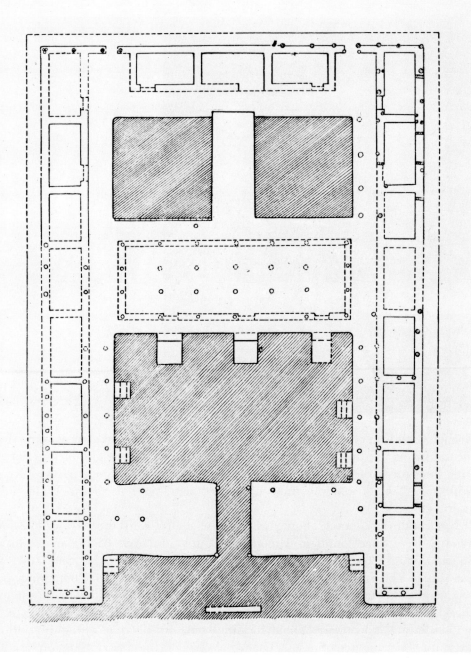

34　Plan of Building 1 at Fengchucun, Qishan County, Shaanxi

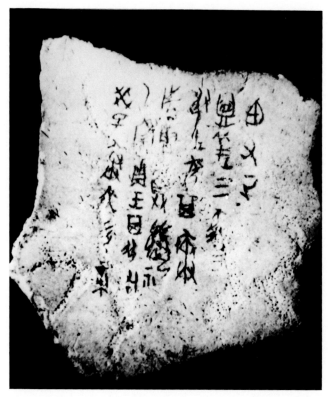

35 Inscriptions on tortoise-shell from the Western Zhou dynasty, found in Building 1 at Fengchucun

sacrifices to Emperor Yi (ca. 1084–1060 B.C.) of the Yin dynasty and for success in his hunting activities and his attacks on the neighbouring states, with the names of ministers of the early Zhou dynasty such as the Great Minister (Dabao) and the duke of Bi and with symbols of the Eight Trigrams (fig. 35).

Inscriptions on oracle bones or tortoise-shells from the Western Zhou dynasty were once found in Hongtong County, Shanxi, Chang'an County, Shaanxi, and Changping County, Beijing; but they were very few in quantity. The inscriptions on tortoise-shells discovered in Changping are very similar to those found at Zhouyuan. Both are provided with square chiselled depressions, and their styles of calligraphy are very much alike. Some characters are as small as a millet seed, displaying a highly skilled inscription-carving technique. The discovery of the inscriptions on oracle bones or tortoise-shells from the Western Zhou dynasty is undoubtedly important, and it has not only helped to identify the nature of the ruins at Zhouyuan but has also opened up a new path for the study of the Western Zhou history.

44

13. *Hoarded Bronze Vessels of the Western Zhou Dynasty*

In ancient times, people often buried their money and valuables underground for various reasons, which is why we find hoarded objects dating from different periods. The storage pits of bronze vessels of the Western Zhou dynasty are of this kind.

In Kazuo County, Liaoning Province, hoards of bronzeware have been discovered time and again. As early as 1955, over ten bronze objects including a food container (*yu*) of the marquis of Yan were found. Then three other hoards were found one after another in 1973 and 1974. Judging from the shapes of the articles, their clan badges, and inscriptions, we can determine that they originated in the period not later than the early Western Zhou dynasty. This hoarded bronzeware was related to the activities of the state of Yan in the early Western Zhou dynasty, which shows that either the influence of Yan had already reached this area by that time or these bronzes were brought there at a later time.

The Guanzhong area in Shaanxi is a place where a large quantity of bronzeware has been found. In 1976 a *guǐ* food container made by an officer called Li was discovered in a pit in Lintong County. The vessel, placed on a square stand, has two lugs in the shape of animal heads with two horns. The body itself as well as the square stand is decorated with patterns of animal faces (fig. 36). On the vessel is an inscription which runs as follows: "Emperor Wu vanquished the Shang dynasty on the day called *jiazi*, and seven days later, the metal with which the vessel was made was given by the emperor as a reward." This is the only inscription on a bronze object from the early Zhou dynasty which describes the expedition against the Yin dynasty. The vessel is the earliest item of bronze of the Western Zhou dynasty discovered so far.

Hoarded bronzes of the Western Zhou dynasty have mostly been discovered in Zhouyuan, Shaanxi. No less than ten discoveries have been made there since the 1960s. Most of the finds consist of vessels of the middle and the late Western Zhou dynasty, which were very likely buried by the royal families as they fled in utter confusion in the last years of the Western Zhou dynasty when the Western Rong* intruded.

The most important find in Zhouyuan is a group of bronzes, discovered in 1976, belonging to the Weishi clan, at Zhuangbaicun in Fufeng County

---

* The northern barbarians, that is, the non-Han tribal people who lived in the northern part of present-day Shaanxi Province during the Western Zhou dynasty.

36 Bronze *guǐ* food container made by Li, found in Lintong County, Shaanxi

37 A group of bronzes belonging to the Weishi clan, discovered at Zhuangbaicun, Fufeng County, Shaanxi

38 Inscribed bronze basin of Qiang found at Zhuangbaicun

39 Bronze wine vessel of Qiu
Wei unearthed at Dongjia,
Qishan County, Shaanxi

47

(fig. 37). This group of bronzes totals 103 pieces. Among them 74 were inscribed, and 55 articles can be identified as the belongings of this clan with the names of clan chiefs of four generations: Zhe, Feng, Qiang, and Xing. The basin of Qiang is the most precious (fig. 38), its inscription bearing 284 characters. The first half of the inscription eulogizes the outstanding achievements made by the Western Zhou emperors, Wen, Wu, Chen, Kang, Zhao, and Mu; the second half describes the family histories of the successive generations. It has provided important material for the study of Western Zhou history. From the inscription on the basin, we can determine that this vessel existed in the times of Emperor Gong (927–908 B.C.) and, in turn, find out the years during which the vessels of the other generations appeared, thus providing a fairly reliable criterion for dating the bronzes of the Western Zhou dynasty.

Among the thirty-seven bronzes of the middle and the late Western Zhou dynasty unearthed at Dongjia in Qishan County in 1975, four vessels of Qiu Wei (fig. 39) and a Ying ewer (*yi*) are of the greatest importance. The long inscriptions of the four vessels record how a low-ranking officer Qiu Wei and a noble named Li started legal proceedings in connection with a compensation payment for land and finally drew a land boundary, and how another noble, the count of Ju, got a jade tablet (*zhang*) and a vehicle from Qiu Wei and gave lands and forests as compensation. The inscription on the Ying ewer is a final verdict in the case between a noble named Ying and his inferior cowherds. The above-mentioned inscriptions have provided some excellent insights into the situation with regard to land relations, lawsuits, and punishments during the middle and the late Western Zhou dynasty.

14. Tombs of the Western Zhou Dynasty

Tombs of the Western Zhou dynasty have been found over a vast area extending westwards to Gansu, eastwards to the coast, northwards to Liaoning, and southwards to Jiangsu. The group of tombs unearthed in Chang'an County, Shaanxi, in the 1950s has been systematically periodized. In recent years some more important tombs have been found in various places.

A graveyard of the state of Yan of the Western Zhou dynasty has been discovered near Liulihe in Fangshan County, Beijing. The tombs all have rectangular pits. Some larger tombs have two passageways, one to the south and the other to the north. The arrangement and grave-goods of these tombs are not much different from those unearthed in the Central Plains. The inscriptions on the bronzes in these tombs sometimes indicate that they were made as rewards granted by the marquis of Yan. The pottery unearthed is very finely made, with patterns of animal faces incised on its polished surface. Glazed pottery has also been found in these tombs.

In Changping County, not far from Liulihe, three wooden-chamber tombs were discovered, in which both inscribed tortoise-shells and bronze weapons were found. Some daggers have their hilts shaped like horse or hawk heads, and some knives also have hawk-head hilts (fig. 40). These weapons are characteristic of the Steppe culture in the north.

The tombs of the Western Zhou dynasty discovered to the south-east in the lower reaches of the Yangtze River have their own features. Most of them have no chambers. Instead, the ground is first paved with a layer of cobblestones on which the coffin and grave-goods are then laid, earth being finally piled on top. Many of the grave-goods are glazed and impressed pottery (or stoneware). Glazed pottery (stoneware or rather proto-porcelain) has also been discovered in the Western Zhou tombs in some other areas but it is far less abundant than in the south-eastern region, which indicates that glazed pottery most likely originated in this region.

In Lingtai County, Gansu, a group of tombs of the Western Zhou dynasty has also been discovered. Two of them, Tombs 1 and 2 at Baicaopo, contain an abundance of grave-goods. The inscriptions on the bronzeware indicate that the dead were the count of Hei and the count of Yuan. Besides complete sets of bronze ceremonial vessels, large numbers of weapons were found, including a dagger with a wooden scabbard. The wood had already decayed but the bronze ornaments with openwork patterns of cows, snakes, and entwined branches remained (fig. 41). There is also a halberd, the shaft socket of which is shaped like a man's head with bushy eyebrows, big

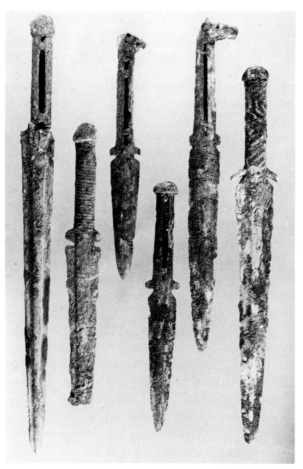

40 Bronze daggers unearthed from a Western Zhou dynasty tomb at Paifu, Changping County, Beijing

eyes, dishevelled hair, and curly beard, or the image of Qiang* or Rong** people.

Two tombs have been found at Rujiazhuang, Baoji, Shaanxi. Both of them have a sloping passageway and human funerary sacrifices. From the inscriptions on the bronzes in the tombs, the dead have been identified as the count of Qiang and his wife Jingji. Complete sets of bronze ceremonial vessels have been found in the tombs, but some of them are quite different from those of the Western Zhou dynasty in style, possibly representing a different culture. In addition, more than thirteen hundred jade articles have been unearthed, among which are carved animals such as deer, tigers, fish, and birds as well as necklaces and beads including glass ones.

* The western barbarians, that is, the non-Han tribal people who lived in the eastern part of present-day Gansu Province during the Western Zhou dynasty.
** See the footnote in p. 45.

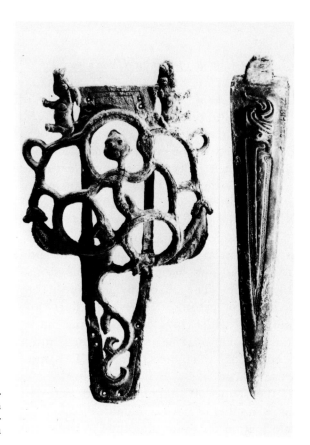

41 Bronze dagger with a scabbard unearthed from a Western Zhou dynasty tomb at Baicaopo, Lingtai County, Gansu

Many Western Zhou tombs have been unearthed in Zhouyuan, Feng, and Gao over the years. In the small- and medium-sized tombs, only pottery was found. The early pottery tripods with long, bulky legs have their own distinguishing features. From the tombs in Zhouyuan, a bronze decoration like a human face was unearthed, presumably a shield boss. A kind of halberd was also found. It has featherlike openwork decorations and is inlaid with turquoises. These halberds were probably meant to be carried by guards of honour rather than for practical use.

Chariots and horses were often buried with the dead in the Western Zhou tombs, and therefore pits used for this purpose have been found in various places. In many cases, the chariot fittings and horse harness were made of bronze. The discoveries will be very useful in the study of the means of transportation at that time.

51

15. The Capital of Jin in Houma and the Capital of Chu in Jiangling

Jin and Chu were two major states during the Spring and Autumn (770–476 B.C.) and Warring States (475–221 B.C.) periods. Chinese archaeologists have excavated large quantities of cultural remains from the Eastern Zhou dynasty in the city of Houma, Shanxi, and at Jinan, Jiangling County, Hubei, which reflect the cultural features of these two states.

In the vicinity of Houma, an ancient city of the Spring and Autumn period was discovered in 1956. Research has established that it was Xintian, the capital of the state of Jin during the latter part of its rule. A fairly large bronze foundry was found in the southern suburbs of the city with a large number of moulds and bronze ingots. The ingots, 110 in number and weighing 191 kilograms, were found neatly piled in a storage pit. They had obviously been brought in from somewhere else to be used for casting. More than thirty thousand fragments of moulds were found, of which over one thousand have been identified as belonging to moulds for bronze ceremonial vessels, musical instruments, weapons, chariot decorations, and horse harness. Two moulds for the legs of a bronze tray were shaped like a man supporting the tray (fig. 42). Another mould is in the shape of an animal head with very fine engraved patterns. The large number of pottery moulds discovered in Houma will provide important information for understanding the technology of bronze casting at that time.

In the south-eastern suburbs of Houma, remains were unearthed of a site for taking oaths of alliance. Over four hundred rectangular pits were found where sacrificial animals such as oxen, horses, and sheep had been buried. In thirty-nine of them, thousands of thin pieces of jade were found, bearing oaths of alliance written with vermilion. Most of them are in the shape of a tablet and some of them are round or of other shapes. The biggest piece is 32 centimetres in length, and the largest number of characters written on one piece is more than two hundred. A fairly complete oath of alliance shows that it was a pledge given by a noble named Yang of the Zhao clan of the state of Jin after he had defeated the Fan and the Zhonghang clans in a power struggle after 497 B.C. It gives some indication of the internal political struggle in the state of Jin during the latter part of the Spring and Autumn period.

Jinan was the capital of Chu. It measures 4.5 kilometres from east to west and 3.5 kilometres from north to south. The remains of a large number of rammed-earth platforms have been found inside the city. Of the many tombs of the Eastern Zhou dynasty outside the city, several larger ones have been unearthed at Wangshan, Tengdian, and some other places.

42 Moulds for the legs of a bronze tray unearthed at Houma, Shanxi

These tombs have very big mounds and rectangular pits with a sloping passageway towards the east. At the bottom of each tomb is a wooden chamber divided into the main chamber where the coffin and one or two outer coffins are put, and wing-chambers where grave-goods are kept.

All these tombs have an abundance of grave-goods. Two swords of the rulers of the state of Yue were unearthed from Wangshan Tomb 1 and Tengdian Tomb 1 respectively. The one from Wangshan Tomb 1 belonged to King Goujian. Its hilt is inlaid with blue glass and turquoises, and its blade is covered with veiled rhombic patterns, on which are superimposed eight characters in bird script (so called because it resembles stylized figures of birds) (fig. 43). The other sword from Tengdian Tomb 1 belonged to King Zhouju. It is inlaid with a gold inscription in bird script. That the two swords of the Yue rulers were unearthed in the tombs of the state of Chu indicates that they might have been trophies of Chu when it defeated Yue.

From Wangshan Tomb 1 was unearthed a large gold-inlaid bronze buckle, 46.2 centimetres long. Its hook is like a dragon head and its obverse is inlaid with gold phoenix designs. It is a very exquisite work of art.

43 Sword of King Goujian of Yue
unearthed from Tomb 1 (a Chu
state tomb) at Wangshan,
Jiangling County, Hubei

A large quantity of lacquerware was unearthed in the same tomb. One piece is a small multi-coloured carved wooden screen, 51.8 centimetres in length. Its base is a relief sculpture of many entwined snakes, and the screen itself is decorated with openwork figures of deer and phoenixes. The whole screen has a black background with colour paintings superimposed (fig. 44). Also unearthed was a carved wooden animal, the

54

44   Multi-coloured carved wooden screen from Wangshan Tomb 1

guardian of the tomb.   It is a strange animal with two heads, two bodies, and four big deer horns, standing on a square pedestal.   The height of the object is 132 centimetres.   It also has a black background with red designs painted on it.   The same type of wooden animal was also found in a tomb in Xinyang, Henan (pl. 8).   In most tombs of the state of Chu, including those found in Changsha, Hunan and some other places, there are many wooden articles as well as lacquerware which is a feature of Chu culture.

16. The Mystery of the State of Zeng: The Tomb of the Marquis Yi of Zeng

Towards the end of the Western Zhou dynasty, the Western Rong, allied with the states of Shen and Zeng, toppled the rule of that dynasty. Where was the state of Zeng situated? The state of Shen is generally believed to be in today's Nanyang, Henan, and, by inference, the state of Zeng ought to be somewhere in its vicinity. But this has never been confirmed and the exact locality of the state of Zeng has been a mystery for over two thousand years.

In 1966 a number of bronze ceremonial vessels of the late Western Zhou dynasty or the early Spring and Autumn period were found in Jingshan County, Hubei. Six of them can be established as belonging to the state of Zeng on the basis of the inscriptions on them. Afterwards more bronzes with the inscriptions of the name of the state of Zeng were found in Xinye County, Henan, and Sui and Zaoyang Counties, Hubei, which has helped to delineate the boundaries of the state of Zeng.

The discovery in Sui County in 1978 of the tomb of the Marquis Yi of the state of Zeng was the climax of the series of discoveries mentioned above. The tomb, occupying an area of 220 square metres, has a vertical pit and a wooden coffin chamber. It has no passageway. Charcoal and whitish clay were piled around the coffin chamber and on top of it.

The chamber is divided into four compartments. In the compartment to the east is kept the coffin of the Marquis Yi, which has an outer coffin made of planks fitted into a framework of bronze posts. The outer coffin is painted black and decorated with red patterns. In the east and west compartments are the wooden coffins of twenty-one immolated persons, all identified as young girls. The middle compartment holds mainly ceremonial vessels and musical instruments, while the north compartment contains weapons, chariot, and horse harness.

More than seven thousand funerary objects were found in the tomb of the Marquis Yi. The most outstanding among them are the musical instruments, in particular, a set of bronze chime-bells consisting of sixty-four bronze bells and one large bell. They were found hanging in three rows on wooden beams supported at both ends by six bronze warriors wearing swords (pl. 9). The whole set of bells weighs 2.5 tons and they were found in very good condition in spite of a lapse of over two thousand years. The bells have inscriptions indicating the temperament and scale. In addition, stone chimes, zitherlike instruments of *qin* and *se*, drums, and pan-pipes were also found. They are all valuable materials for the study of the music of the pre-Qin period.

45 A pair of bronze vessels for cooling wine, unearthed from the tomb of the Marquis Yi of Zeng in Sui County, Hubei

46 Bronze vessel with a bronze basin as its stand unearthed from the tomb of the Marquis Yi of Zeng

Many ceremonial bronze vessels were found in the tomb. Most noteworthy is a pair of exquisitely wrought vessels for cooling wine. The pair consists of a square vessel with a square pot inside, which is hooked to the bottom of the square vessel (fig. 45). The vessel has a lid with a square hole in the middle coinciding with the rim of the interior pot which in turn has a square lid of its own. Ice could be put between the vessel and the pot. Also noteworthy is a bronze vessel (*zun*) with a bronze basin as its stand (fig. 46). Both have a fretwork of interwoven *chi*-snakes and gargoyles decorating their rims. The decorations were presumably the product of the lost wax process, which was an important innovation in the technology of bronze casting.

The grave-goods included much lacquerware and jade and gold articles such as gold cups, jade pendants, and lacquerware food containers with lids. They are all rare masterpieces.

It was possible to determine the date of the tomb from the inscription on the large bronze bell included in the grave-goods. The bell was cast in honour of the Marquis Yi of Zeng in the fifty-sixth year of the reign of King Hui of Chu (433 B.C.). The tomb must have been built, therefore, somewhat later than 433 B.C. Since the date of the tomb and the identity of the dead man have been established and the grave-goods are abundant and in good condition, the tomb can be considered a typical one of a marquis during the early Warring States period.

17. The Discovery of the Tomb of the King of the State of Zhongshan

The tomb of the king of the state of Zhongshan, excavated since 1974 in Pingshan County, Hebei, is the only one that has been established as belonging to a king of the Warring States period.

The state of Zhongshan was founded by a tribe called Baidi during the Warring States period. Its power was next only to the seven powerful states of the period, but the recorded history of this state has been scanty. The discovery of the tomb is, therefore, of particular importance.

Pingshan Tomb 1, the tomb of Cuo, the fifth king of the state of Zhongshan, has a rectangular pit with two passageways, one to the south and the other to the north. The whole tomb is 110 metres long. It has a very big mound with three flights of steps. On the top of the mound there were remains of ruined funerary temples with a winding corridor and an apron. In front of the tomb is a pair of pits for chariots and horses, one pit on each side, and there is another pit for boats on the west side. Inside the tomb, there is a coffin chamber with two store-rooms for the funeral objects on the east side and one on the west side. The coffin chamber has been robbed and burned down, but the store-rooms are intact. A large number of objects have been unearthed there.

The most important discovery in the coffin chamber was a bronze plate or plaque 94×48×1 cm, showing the plan of the tomb. On one side is a pair of door knockers in the shape of animal heads, while on the other there is a gold- and silver-inlaid plan showing the surrounding walls of the mausoleum, the funerary temples of the king and queen, and a decree of the king (fig. 47). In the light of the plan and the arrangement of Tomb 1, a restoration of the original tomb has been worked out (fig. 48), which illustrates the burial system of the Warring States period.

Of the large quantity of bronzes unearthed in the two store-rooms, three items have long inscriptions. One is a big bronze tripod with iron legs, its inscription consisting of 469 characters; another is a square pot (*fanghu*) with dragon designs, its inscription consisting of 450 characters. Both objects were made in the fourteenth year of the reign of King Cuo (309 or 308 B.C.). Yet another bronze item is a round pot (*hu*) with an inscription of 182 characters, which was engraved on the pot by King Qie Ci who succeeded to the throne after the death of King Cuo. All three inscriptions describe the episode when, as a result of the abdication by King Kuai of the state of Yan to his Prime Minister Zi Zhi in 316 B.C., the state was thrown into great disorder and its capital was captured by the state of Qi, and when the state of Zhongshan, taking advantage of the situation, attacked Yan,

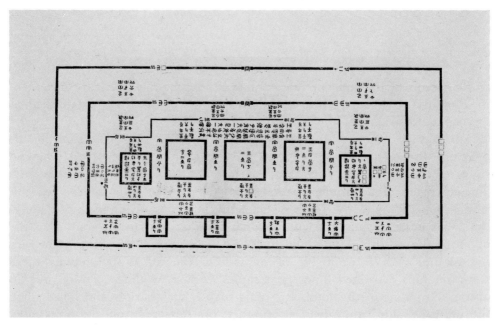

47 Plan of the funeral temples above the tomb of King Cuo of the state of Zhongshan as inscribed on the bronze plate unearthed from his tomb in Pingshan County, Hebei

48 Reconstruction of the funeral temples above the tomb of King Cuo

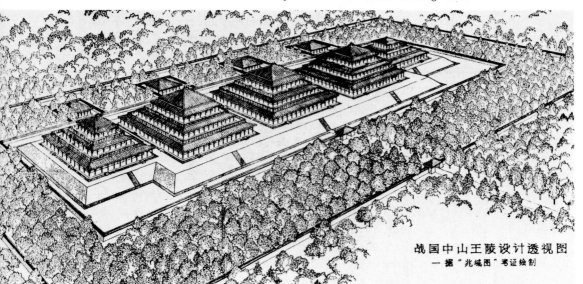

战国中山王陵设计透视图
——据"兆域图"考证绘制

49 Square bronze table decorated with dragon and phoenix patterns, unearthed from the tomb of King Cuo

occupied a large area of the state several hundred *li** deep and captured scores of cities. The inscriptions also sing the praises to Premier Zhou of the state of Zhongshan. These inscriptions have provided very useful documentation as regards the history of this state.

From this tomb a large number of bronze objects inlaid with gold and silver have been unearthed. They are vividly shaped and are decorated with exceptionally fine patterns, which is a clear indication of the state of the art of metal casting and the plastic arts. One of the objects unearthed was a square bronze table (fig. 49). Its base is a bronze ring supported by four small sikas. On the ring stand four dragons and four phoenixes, the dragons holding up their heads and the phoenixes spreading their wings, their bodies and wings intertwined. The dragons' heads rest against four blocks, which in turn support the four corners of the table. The table is decorated with gold- and silver-inlaid patterns. The exquisiteness of the table is matchless.

---

* A *li* is an ancient Chinese unit of length equal to about half a kilometre.

61

50 Bronze lamp with fifteen oil-cups unearthed from the tomb of King Cuo

Also unearthed was a lamp with fifteen oil-cups (fig. 50). It is 84.5 centimetres high, made up of eight sections. On its branches monkeys are playing, and on the stand, two men, stripped to the waist, are teasing them with food. The images are very vivid and lifelike. In addition, there were also found a bronze tiger holding a deer in its mouth (fig. 51), a two-winged supernatural animal, a wine vessel in the shape of an ox with a hole in its back, a lamp shaped like a human figure, and so forth, which are all rare masterpieces.

62

51 Bronze tiger holding a deer in its mouth decorated with gold- and silver-inlaid patterns, unearthed from the tomb of King Cuo

52 Bronze object shaped like the Chinese character *shan* 山 (mountain), unearthed from the tomb of King Cuo

Also found in the tomb was a bronze object shaped like the Chinese character *shan* 山 (mountain) (fig. 52). The top part of the object consists of three parallel spearheads and its base has a socket into which a shaft can be fitted. The object is 1.48 metres in height. Objects like this have never been found before. Presumably it was used as an insignia of rank carried in procession.

The discovery of the tomb of the king of Zhongshan has filled some of the lacunae in the history and culture of the state of Zhongshan. As the remains of the state of Zhongshan are further unearthed, we will have a better and clearer idea of what the state of Zhongshan was like.

18. Pottery Figures of Warriors and Horses in the Tomb of Emperor Qin Shihuang

Qin Shihuang, the First Emperor (259–210 B.C.) of the Qin dynasty, was a famous emperor in the history of China. He united the country which had been divided and torn apart by warring states, and he established the Qin dynasty (221–207 B.C.). His tomb is in today's Lintong County, Shaanxi, with Mount Li to its south and the Wei River to its north. It was an extremely magnificent tomb, for even now there exists on the ground a big mound of rammed earth, 76 metres in height, with a foundation measuring 485 by 515 metres. The tomb has two walls. The inner wall is a square with a perimeter of 2,525.4 metres, while the outer wall is a rectangle with a perimeter of 6,294 metres. In 1961 the tomb was listed as one of the major ancient monuments under the protection of the state.

In 1974 a huge pit filled with pottery figures was found 1,225 metres to the east of the outer wall of the emperor's tomb. From March 1974 to the end of 1977, altogether three pits were found. Pit 1 has an area of up to 12,000 square metres. The total excavated area of the three pits is so far 2,500 square metres, and the unearthed objects include some 800 pottery figures of warriors, 124 pottery horses, 18 wooden chariots, and more than 9,000 weapons of various types. Without any doubt, this was an unprecedented discovery in the history of Chinese archaeology.

The pits where the figures of the warriors were buried had all been built according to the same pattern, the floor being paved with bricks and the ceiling being supported by wooden beams. The pottery figures were arranged in the battle formation of the time, which consisted of infantrymen interspersed with chariots. Because some parts of the vault had been destroyed by fire and the ceiling of some other parts had collapsed, some figures were broken when unearthed, and, in particular, most of the wooden chariots had already decayed and only vestiges remained.

The pottery figures include infantrymen, horsemen, charioteers, and officers. The soldiers are all between 1.75 and 1.90 metres tall while the officers are as tall as 1.96 metres. Some of the infantrymen wear robes; others are in armour (fig. 53). They carry swords, knives, spears, crossbows, etc. Some soldiers in armour are kneeling on one knee, with both hands holding a bow. The horsemen are all wearing short armour which reaches only down to the waist, possibly to make riding easier. The charioteers have their hands raised as if holding reins. The robes and armour of the officers are different from those of the soldiers. In particular, their tall hats with two feathers give an indication of their special status. The horses are generally

53 Pottery figure unearthed from the tomb of Emperor Qin Shihuang in Lintong County, Shaanxi

66

2 metres long and 1.5 metres high. The horses are well modelled, especially their heads which seem very lifelike.

The pottery figures were made by first fashioning a rough model out of clay strips over which fine clay was then laid and shaped into eyebrows, eyes, hair, clothes, hats, and decorations, and finally painted in red, green, black, yellow, etc. The colours had almost gone, but they can be restored.

The pottery figures of warriors and horses in the funerary pits of Emperor Qin Shihuang's tomb occupy an extremely important place in the history of ancient Chinese sculpture. They represented the best standards of pottery sculpture of the time. Their realistic approach and simple style, which characterized ancient Chinese sculpture, influenced all subsequent art and established a tradition in Chinese sculpture.

19. The City of Chang'an in the Han Dynasty and the City of Luoyang in the Eastern Han and Wei Dynasties

The site of the city of Chang'an, the capital of the Western Han dynasty (206 B.C.–A.D. 24), is situated about 10 kilometres to the north-west of present-day Xi'an. Isolated parts of the rammed-earth city walls can be seen from afar towering into the air.

Archaeological study of the city began in 1956. Since then, its walls, streets, and palace sites have been surveyed and four city gates have been excavated. In 1975 the site of an armoury was found. Two sites of ceremonial buildings of the Han dynasty have also been found in the southern suburbs of the city. The study is continuing according to plan as an important part of the archaeological research into the Han dynasty.

54 Plan of the Han dynasty capital Chang'an

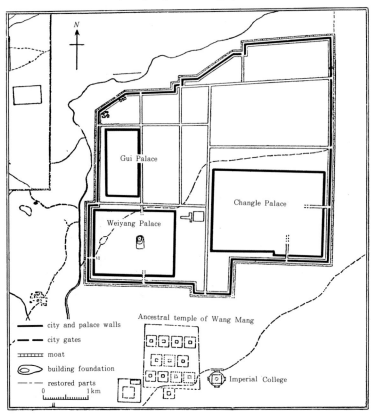

68

The city of Chang'an was built in the third century B.C. As the city walls were built after the palaces had been constructed, they had to fit in with the palaces and the terrain, and therefore zigzagged in some places. According to our survey, the east wall is approximately 6,000 metres long, the south wall 7,600 metres, the west wall 4,900 metres, and the north wall 7,200 metres, totalling 25,700 metres. The total area of the city is 36 square kilometres. There are altogether twelve gates, three to each wall (fig. 54). Each gateway has three clear openings, each of which is wide enough to allow four chariots to pass abreast. Some ruts have been found (fig. 55). Most of the gates were destroyed by fire. Some of them were rebuilt and were in use until the sixth century A.D.

There were eight main streets inside the city. Palaces occupied more than half of the city area. The remains of the front hall of the famous Weiyang Palace can be seen towering above the ground even now, measuring 350 metres in length, 200 metres in width, and 15 metres in height at its highest point located at its northern end (fig. 56).

55   Ruins of the Xuanping Gate from the Han dynasty capital Chang'an, near present-day Xi'an

56　Ruins of the Weiyang Palace from the Han dynasty capital Chang'an

East of the Weiyang Palace was an armoury, 800 metres long by 320 metres wide, which had seven store-rooms, the largest one being subdivided into four compartments. What has remained of the weapons includes iron armour, halberds, spears, swords, knives, arrowheads, and bronze arrowheads and dagger-axes. Excavations have proved that the armoury, like the other buildings inside the city, was also destroyed by the flames of war towards the end of the rule of Wang Mang at the beginning of the first century A.D.

One of the two ceremonial buildings unearthed in the southern suburbs of Chang'an is a square hall on a round foundation in the middle of a big square courtyard which has four walls, each with a gate, and is surrounded by a moat. The hall is the main body of the compound. It could be the Instruction Hall of the Imperial College of the time (fig. 57). There is another building to the west of it, differently arranged, which is possibly the site of the Nine Shrines of the temple of royal ancestors.

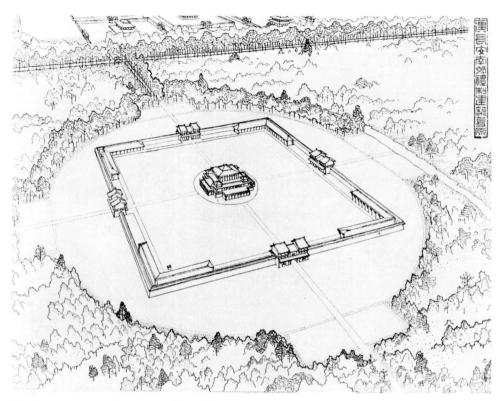

57 Reconstruction of a ceremonial building in the southern suburbs of Chang'an

The city of Luoyang, the capital of the Eastern Han dynasty (A.D. 25–220), is situated approximately 15 kilometres to the east of today's Luoyang, Henan. The city was a capital for more than five hundred years, from the time of the Eastern Han dynasty in the early first century A.D. through the Wei and Western Jin dynasties and into the Northern Wei dynasty in the mid-sixth century.

The archaeological study of the city has so far included a survey of the city walls and gates, excavations of the foundation of the famous pagoda of the Yongning Temple of the Northern Wei dynasty (423–534) and the official residences inside the city, and excavations of the Observatory, the Instruction Hall, and the student's quarter of the Imperial College in the southern suburbs (fig. 58).

The city walls were also made of rammed earth. According to the survey, the remains of the east, west, and north walls are 3,900, 3,400, and 2,700 metres long respectively. The south wall was washed away by

71

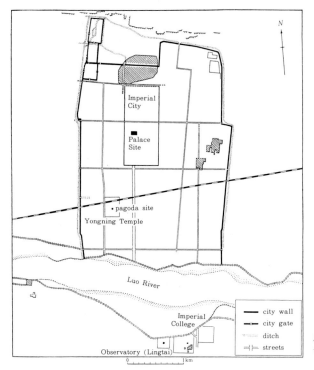

58 Plan of the capital Luoyang in
the Eastern Han and Wei dynasties

floods, but the distance between the southern ends of the east wall and the
west wall shows that its length would have been 2,460 metres. The city
walls form a rectangle. There are twelve gates as in Chang'an but they
are not distributed evenly on the four sides. Instead, the north wall has
two gates, and the south wall four gates. At the north-west corner of the
city, a fort was built during the Wei dynasty (220–65). It forms a very
special complex.

The city had twenty-four main streets and two palaces, the South Palace
and the North Palace. The South Palace was abandoned during the
Northern Wei dynasty and a new palace was built on the foundations
of the North Palace of the Eastern Han dynasty. This meant that the
palaces were no longer scattered as they had been since the Han dynasty,
a fact which had a great influence on city planning thereafter.

The Observatory, which was called Lingtai in the Eastern Han dynasty,
is situated to the west of the highway outside the south gate, facing the
site of the Instruction Hall to its east. The Observatory is enclosed by
walls and has a square platform of about 50 square metres, on which astro-

59　Site of Observatory (Lingtai) in the Eastern Han dynasty capital Luoyang, Henan

nomical observations were made. What remains of the platform is about 8 metres high (fig. 59). Around the platform some structures were built, the floors of which were paved with rectangular bricks, and the four sides of the platform were painted blue on the surface in the east side, white in the west, red in the south, and black in the north. The design was apparently based on the theory of five elements, in which the four gods, that is, the blue dragon, white tiger, red bird, and black *xuanwu* which is composed of a tortoise and a snake, represented the four cardinal points. The site is so far the earliest observatory discovered in China.

Of the tombs from the Han dynasty which have been excavated during the past few years, the most important are the Mawangdui tombs in Changsha, Hunan, and the Mancheng tombs in Mancheng County, Hebei.

Tomb 1 at Mawangdui was excavated in 1972, and Tombs 2 and 3 in 1973. The unearthed seals, clay sealings, and the inscriptions on the unearthed lacquerware have proved that Tomb 2 is the tomb of Licang, the marquis of Dai and concurrently the prime minister of Changsha; Tomb 1 is that of his wife; and Tomb 3 may be that of his son. They were buried between 186 and 168 B.C.

The three are all pit tombs with wooden chambers. Tomb 1, which is in the best state of preservation, has four coffins in the funerary chamber, one inside the other (fig. 60). This explains why the remains of the wife of Licang are fairly well preserved. Incidentally the news of the discovery created quite a furore when it was published. Tomb 2 has been robbed. Two thousand or so cultural relics have been unearthed from Tombs 1 and 3; among them silk fabrics and lacquerware, which are especially well preserved, have been found. There are also silk paintings, books written on silk, and different sorts of food offerings. The wooden strips found in Tomb 1 are inscribed with a list of funeral objects. The unearthed relics give some idea of the habits and customs of the aristocracy of the Han dynasty.

The silk clothing includes clothes of plain silk, a gown of vermilion-coloured gauze (pl. 10), silk painted and printed with coloured patterns, yellow silk embroidered with the longevity (*changshou*) pattern (pl. 11), yellow monochrome figured silk embroidered with the riding-on-clouds (*chengyun*) pattern, and silk embroidered with the chessboard pattern; all are distinguished by the fineness of the designs and their bright colours. Among the lacquerware are tripods, pot (*hu*) (pl. 12), square wine vessels (*fang*), caskets (*he*), small cups, basins, ewers, trays (*an*) (pl. 13), and so forth, which, when unearthed, were bright and clean and in perfect condition.

The coffins in Tombs 1 and 3 are each covered with a silk painting. The painting in Tomb 1 is T-shaped and 2.05 metres long. Its upper part portrays the sun and the moon which symbolize the heavens, whereas its lower part depicts some strange animals which symbolize the sea. In between, there is a portrait of an old lady, probably the very lady lying in the coffin, symbolizing the earth (pl. 14). The silk painting in Tomb 3 is nearly the same except that in the middle there is a man instead of a lady. In the coffin of Tomb 3 there are also other silk paintings, such

60   Coffin and outer coffins of Mawangdui Tomb 1 in Changsha, Hunan

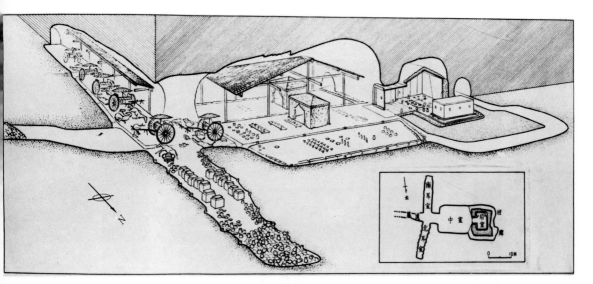

61 Reconstruction of Mancheng Tomb 1 (Liu Sheng's tomb) from the Han dynasty in Hebei

as *A Guard of Honour with Chariots and Horses* and diagrams of physical exercises.

Unearthed from Tomb 3 were a large number of silk books including *Laozi*, *The Book of Changes* (*Yijing*), *Records of the Warring States* (*Zhanguo ce*), *Discourses and Anecdotes from the Spring and Autumn Period* (*Chunqiu shiyu*), *Studies of Horses* (*Xiangma jing*), and *Fifty-two Prescriptions* (*Wushier bingfang*), as well as writings and paintings about astronomy and geography. These are very important documents in the fields of palaeography, history, philosophy, and the history of science and technology.

The Mancheng tombs from the Han dynasty, excavated in 1968, were the tombs of Liu Sheng, prince of Zhongshan of the Western Han dynasty, and his wife Dou Wan. Liu Sheng died in 113 B.C. The tombs were hewn into the cliff of a hill. Liu Sheng's tomb is 51.7 metres long, 37.5 metres wide, and 6.8 metres high. Its construction is modelled on that of a palace, with a front hall, back chamber, and a side-chamber on each flank. The front hall was originally a tile-roofed wooden house and the back chamber was encircled by a corridor. All this is compatible with the status of a prince (fig. 61). The two tombs contain more than four thousand funeral objects, the best known being some finely crafted bronze objects and two jade suits sewn with fine gold threads.

Variegated in pattern and resplendent in colour, the gilded small-mouthed jar with coiled-dragon design, the gilded small-mouthed jar with decorative

76

62 Brick with paintings found in the tomb of the Wei and Jin dynasties in Jiayuguan, Gansu

bosses, and the gold- and silver-inlaid small-mouthed jar with an inscription in bird script are treasures of Han bronzework. A *boshan* mountain-shaped incense burner with gold inlays unearthed from Liu Sheng's tomb is especially striking (pl. 15). Its lid is cast in the shape of undulating flames and its body inlaid with exquisite gold decorations. The 48-centimetre-high gilded bronze lamp from the Changxing Palace consists of a lantern held by a kneeling court maid. The lamp shade can open and close freely when adjusted, and the smoke enters the body of the maid through her right arm. Its lifelike figurine and ingenious design make it a masterpiece that compels our admiration (pl. 16).

When they were buried, Liu Sheng and Dou Wan were both enshrouded in jade funerary suits sewn with fine gold threads. The suits were in a good state of preservation when discovered and have since been completely restored. Liu Sheng's jade suit is 1.88 metres long and composed of 2,498 small jade plates of different shapes perforated and linked together with 1,100 grams of fine gold threads (pl. 17); his wife's, modelled on a lady's garment, is 1.72 metres long and made up of 2,160 jade plates sewn with 600 grams of gold threads. Jade funerary suits were used exclusively for emperors and high-ranking nobles of the Han dynasty and were sewn with gold, silver, or bronze threads according to the rank of the deceased. The jade suits in the Mancheng tombs were the first such objects ever found and completely restored and they are also the earliest. Several others have been unearthed since then. The latest one is a jade suit sewn with bronze

77

threads found in the tombs of the patriarchal clan of Caocao (the duke of Wei) in Bo County, Anhui Province. At the time of Caopi, the son of Caocao and the first emperor of the Wei dynasty (at the beginning of the third century A.D.), the use of jade suits was prohibited.

Tombs of the Wei (A.D. 220–65), Jin (265–420), and Southern and Northern Dynasties (420–589), though not so big as those of the Han dynasty, have the characteristics of their own times. The brick reliefs in the tombs of the Wei and Jin dynasties excavated in the city of Jiayuguan, Gansu, are considered as simple artistic creations, usually depicting agricultural production, husbandry, fortified villages, and food-growing garrison troops (fig. 62). The lacquer paintings on wooden screens found in the tomb in the city of Datong, Shanxi, from the Northern Wei period, mainly portray historical figures (fig. 63). The style of painting is similar to that of such famous paintings handed down from ancient times as the *Painting of a Morality Tale of Women Officials* (*Nüshizhen tu*), *Painting of Celebrated Women* (*Lienü tu*), and *Painting of Emperors and Kings* (*Diwang tu*). They are all important documents in the history of Chinese painting. There are big brick reliefs instead of wall paintings in the tombs of the Southern Dynasties, for example, the Seven Sages Living in the Bamboo Groves and the brick relief of the story of hermit Rong Qigi representing the Southern style of painting. The most distinctive of the grave-goods in the tombs of the two Jins and the Southern Dynasties are the large quantity of celadon ware. The beautifully shaped celadon lotus vases unearthed in Nanjing and Wuhan are excellent examples of artifacts from that period.

Tombs of the Sui (581–618) and Tang (618–907) dynasties are found throughout China. In the region close to the then capital Chang'an, for example, more than ten thousand tombs have been excavated. Some are very large in scale. For instance, around the Qianling, the mausoleum of Emperor Gaozong and Empress Wu Zetian, the tombs of Princess Yongtai, Crown Prince Yide, and Crown Prince Zhanghuai were also known as "mausoleums" even at that time. The wall paintings in these tombs are most famous. We shall describe three of them in turn; they were all painted in 706.

The first is the *Painting of Maids of Honour* from the tomb of Princess Yongtai. This portrays nine young court maids. The one at the head is standing serenely and the other eight are either holding plates, square caskets, round fans, or horsetail whisks. They are all graceful in manner with long skirts hanging down to the ground, but they vary in facial expression (pl. 18). This is the best wall painting depicting court ladies from the Tang dynasty ever found.

The second is the *Painting of the Imperial Entourage* in the tomb of Crown Prince Yide. It portrays the scene of the entourage when the crown prince

78

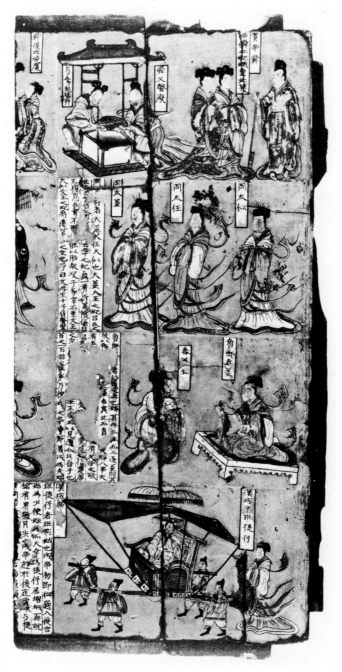

63 Lacquer painting unearthed from the tomb of the Northern
Wei dynasty in Datong, Shanxi

79

64 Wall painting of an imperial entourage from the tomb of Crown Prince Yide in Qian County, Shaanxi

65 Wall painting of a polo game from the tomb of Crown Prince Zhanghuai in Qian County, Shaanxi

makes a tour. The guards of honour are wearing neckless robes and black head-dresses and are armed with swords and bows. Holding high the banners portraying tigers and eagles, they are advancing slowly, some riding horses and some walking (fig. 64).

The third is the *Painting of a Polo Game* in the tomb of Crown Prince Zhanghuai. Five polo-players, each riding a fine horse and with a polo-stick in their hands, are competing with each other. One of them, swinging his polo-stick at his side, is about to hit the ball. The strong and vigorous players and prancing horses present a vivid picture of the excitement of the game (fig. 65).

The grave-goods found in the tombs of the Sui and Tang dynasties are for the most part pottery and porcelain and include different kinds of pottery figurines. The well-known three-colour pottery figurines of the Tang dynasty have been unearthed mainly from tombs in Xi'an and Luo-yang dating from the height of the Tang dynasty. The figurines are bright in colour and graceful in shape. One of the outstanding finds is the figurine

81

66 Three-colour pottery figurine of a Bactrian camel carrying musicians on its back, from a Tang dynasty tomb in Xi'an

of a Bactrian camel carrying a small group of musicians on its back, unearthed in Xi'an from the tomb of General Xianyu Tinghui who was buried in 723 (fig. 66). Five musicians are playing on a platform on the camel's back. Three of them are Hu* people with deep-set eyes, big noses, and thick beards; perhaps they are playing a piece of popular Hu music.

---

* Hu is the name given to all non-Han peoples who lived in the north and west of China in ancient times.

21. The Cities of Chang'an and Luoyang during the Sui and Tang Dynasties

The sites of the cities of Chang'an and Luoyang—two capitals of the Sui and Tang dynasties—are very extensive and full of relics. A great deal of excavation and study has been achieved on the sites of these two ancient cities during the past twenty years.

The Sui and Tang dynasty city of Chang'an was first constructed in 582 and is located in the present city of Xi'an. Since 1957 a comprehensive exploration has been carried out of the outer walls, streets, residential quarters, markets, the Imperial Palace, and the Imperial City as well as the Daming Palace jutting out from the north-eastern part of the city's northern wall. As a result, the following sites have been excavated: the Linde Hall and Hanyuan Hall of the Daming Palace, the Chongxuan Gate, the Administrative Hall of the Xingqing Palace, the West Market, the East Market, the Mingde Gate, and the Qinglong Monastery.

The outer walls, built of rammed earth, are 9,721 metres long from east to west and 8,651.7 metres long from north to south. The Mingde Gate is the main entrance in the outer southern wall. It has five rectangular entrances, each 5 metres wide and 18.5 metres deep, and is one of the most spectacular gates of Tang dynasty Chang'an. Facing the Mingde Gate is the Zhuque Avenue over 140 metres in width, the main avenue of Chang'an of the Sui and Tang dynasties. A partial exploration of some streets and a study of historical records enabled us to locate all 108 blocks, thus accurately reconstituting the layout of Chang'an (fig. 67).

Situated just outside of the north-eastern part of the northern wall of Tang dynasty Chang'an, the Daming Palace was built in 634. The exploration and survey of the past few years have succeeded in locating its walls, halls, pavilions, lakes, and gardens. What is more, the Hanyuan Hall for audience and the Linde Hall for entertaining officials have also been excavated. The platform base of the Hanyuan Hall is 75.9 metres long from east to west and 41.3 metres long from north to south. The hall itself is about 60 metres long and about 22 metres wide. In front of the platform base, there are three flights of stairs running parallel to one another, each extending 70 metres. The hall is flanked by two pavilions: the Xiangluan and the Xifeng. The platform base of the pavilions is 15 metres above the ground. The rammed-earth base of the Linde Hall is 130.41 metres long from north to south and 77.55 metres wide from east to west, and on it stand three buildings adjoining one another. The hall is flanked by matching pavilions (fig. 68). Architectural historians have restored the two sets of buildings with the help of data and other materials found in the archaeo-

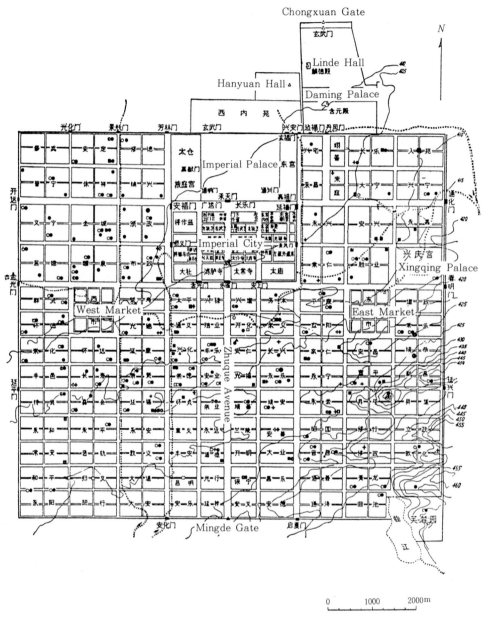

Chongxuan Gate
玄武门

Linde Hall
麟德殿

Hanyuan Hall▲

Daming Palace
含元殿

光化门 景林门 芳林门 玄武门
西 内 苑
安福门 丹凤门
玄福门

太仓

Imperial Palace 东宫

Imperial City

西市 West Market

East Market 东市

Xingqing Palace 兴庆宫

Zhuque Avenue

Mingde Gate 明德门
安化门 启夏门

天坛园

0   1000   2000m

67 Plan of the Tang dynasty capital Chang'an

84

68 The site of the Linde Hall in the Daming Palace of the Tang dynasty in Chang'an, present-day Xi'an

logical excavations. The magnificence of the Hanyuan Hall (fig. 69) and the complexity of the Linde Hall fully reflect the high level of science, technology, and art in the Tang dynasty.

The West Market, one of the two commercial centres of Tang dynasty Chang'an, was also excavated. The sites show that the streets must have been lined with shops and stores. In one place, a large quantity of broken bowls and dishes were found—perhaps the site of a food store. At another place, there were large quantities of ornaments made of bones and jewellery such as glass beads, pearls, agate, and crystal—perhaps the site of a jeweller's shop. At yet another place, potsherds were piled as high as 30 centimetres—probably the site of a pottery shop.

Relics from the Tang dynasty have also been found in the residential quarters of Chang'an. The most outstanding consist of over 270 gold and silver vessels found in a hoard in Xinghua ward (now Hejiacun in the southern suburbs of Xi'an). The shape and design of some vessels bear a resemblance to those of the Sassanian gold and silver vessels of Persia.

A comprehensive survey has been carried out since 1959 of the sites of the city of Luoyang, the eastern capital of the Sui and Tang dynasties,

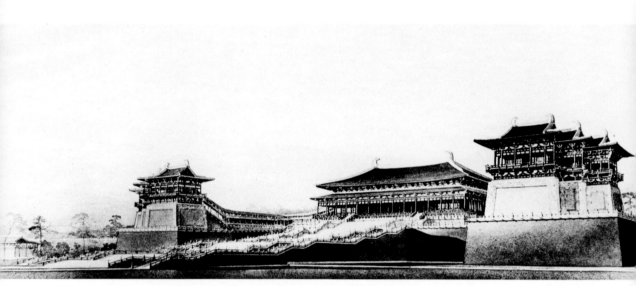

69   Reconstruction of the Hanyuan Hall in the Daming Palace

which lies in the present city of Luoyang. Of its outer walls, the
eastern section is 7,312 metres long, the southern section 7,290 metres long,
the northern section 6,138 metres long, and the western section 6,776 metres
long. The Imperial Palace, the Imperial City, East Town, Yaoyi Town,
Huanbi Town, and Hanjiacang Town have also been located. Though
some blocks of this ancient city were destroyed by the flooding of the Luo
River, its layout can still be reconstituted (fig. 70).

The Youye Gate of the Imperial City was excavated in 1959. The
stratigraphical deposit shows that this gate lasted until the late Northern
Song dynasty (960–1127), when it was burned down by the Jin kingdom
armies. In the west of the Imperial Palace was excavated an octagonal
pavilion. The path leading to it is paved with lotus-patterned square bricks.
More than two hundred subterranean granaries with a diameter of 6 to 18
metres and a depth of 5 to 10 metres were found in Hanjiacang Town in
1971. The specially baked bottom of the pit is as hard as rock. Its bottom
and walls are lined with planks. Decomposed millet seeds have been found
in some granaries. There are also inscriptions carved on the brick recording
the location of the granary, the source of the stored grain, its variety and
quantity, and the date of storage together with the name and official title
of the supervisor responsible. This find has contributed to the study of
the economic situation and of the grain supply of the city of Luoyang, the
eastern capital of the Tang dynasty.

86

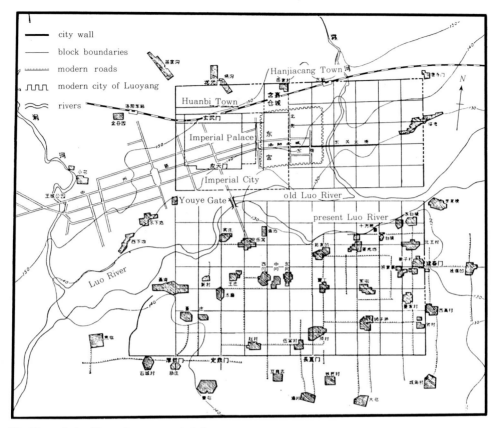

Plan of the Tang dynasty capital Luoyang

Legend:
- city wall
- block boundaries
- modern roads
- modern city of Luoyang
- rivers

Labels on map:
Hanjiacang Town
Huanbi Town
Imperial Palace
Imperial City
Youye Gate
old Luo River
present Luo River
Luo River

70 Plan of the Tang dynasty capital Luoyang

87

22. *Important Discoveries along the "Silk Road"*

Since Zhang Qian travelled to the Western Regions in the second century B.C. (the middle period of the Western Han dynasty), land communication between China and countries to the west of China became frequent. It was along this route that the famous Chinese silks were exported to the Roman Empire. Hence it was called the "Silk Road" by later historians.

The Silk Road began at Chang'an (Xi'an), the capital of the Han and Tang dynasties, traversed the Hexi Corridor of Gansu Province and Xinjiang, then led westwards (fig. 71). The road divided into two at Dunhuang because of the Taklamakan Desert. The southern route ran from Dunhuang, through Loulan (Shanshan, now the north-eastern part of Ruoqiang= Qarkilik), Yutian (now Hetian=Khotan), and Shache (now Yarkand), then across the Pamirs to the Great Yuezhi in the middle part of the Amu River basin in Afghanistan and Parthia (now Iran), going further westwards to such countries as Tiaozhi (now Iraq or Arabia) and Daqin (the Roman Empire). The northern route ran from Dunhuang, through Qoco (Gao-chang, now Turfan), Guizi (now Kuche=Kucha), Shule (now Kashi= Kashgar), then across the Pamirs to Dawan (now Fergana in the Soviet Union), Kangju (Kangkuo, now Samarkand), and further westwards to Daqin through Parthia. The Silk Road became an important route in commercial and cultural exchanges. It remained prosperous for about one thousand years from the second century B.C. to the eighth century A.D. (the middle period of the Tang dynasty).

Along this route passed the exports of Chinese silks to the West and China's imports of silverware, spice, precious stones, glassware, and woollen

71 Sketch map of the Silk Roads to the West

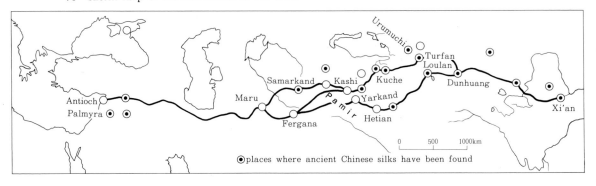

places where ancient Chinese silks have been found

72　Persian brocade found at Astana, Turfan, Xinjiang

fabrics. A large number of cultural relics from the Sassanian dynasty of Persia and the Eastern Roman (Byzantine) Empire have been found in China, and most of them were unearthed along the Silk Road.

In the ancient tombs at Astana in Turfan, Xinjiang, dating from after the seventh century A.D., we have discovered a kind of brocade entirely different from that of the Han and early Tang dynasties. The weaving method is a weft-patterned compound twill weave with a double-yarn warp. The patterns include a Sassanian standing birds design and that of boar's head within a pearl-bordered medallion. This is probably the so-called Persian brocade mentioned in Chinese texts (fig. 72). It was produced in the east of Iran and was widely acclaimed in China after its importation. There are also Chinese imitations of the Persian brocade among the objects found in the ancient tombs at Astana.

Gold and silver vessels of the Sassanian dynasty of ancient Persia were also welcomed in China. The eight-lobed silver bowl with a sea-horse design (fig. 73), unearthed in the hoards of Daicheng of the Northern Wei

73 Eight-lobed silver bowl with a sea-horse design found in Datong, Shanxi

dynasty in Datong, was produced by the Sassanian craftsmen. The three gilded bronze goblets (fig. 74) and one partly gilded silver bowl unearthed in the same place, though not in the Sassanian style, show a distinctive Greek flavour and are undoubtedly the products of Western or Central Asia. Gilded gold and silver cups with stems and silver ewers (fig. 75) made by the Sassanian craftsmen are also found in the tombs of the Sui

74　Gilded bronze goblet found in Datong

dynasty in Xi'an and the Liao dynasty tomb at Aohan Qi, Inner Mongolia. In the hoards of the Tang dynasty in Hejiacun, Xi'an, there are a great quantity of imitations of Sassanian-style gold and silver vessels made by Chinese craftsmen.

From time to time, glass objects of the Sassanian dynasty are discovered in the tombs of the Eastern Jin dynasty in Nanjing. These are thought to have been imported by sea. Among the glass objects imported along the Silk Road, the most important are the glass bowls, goblet, and duck-shaped water-dropper unearthed in the tomb of General Feng Shufu (died in 415) of the state of Northern Yan (409–36) in Beipiao County, Liaoning. These glass objects are thin and transparent and are pale green or dark green in colour. The duck-shaped water-dropper, 5.2 centimetres across its body with a length of 21 centimetres, bears a strong resemblance to the Roman dolphin-shaped glass water-dropper unearthed from the sites of the Kushan Empire at Begram in Afghanistan.

75 Silver ewer found in the Liao
dynasty tomb at Aohan Qi,
Inner Mongolia

With the development of trade, large quantities of silver coins of the
Sassanian dynasty and gold coins of the Eastern Roman Empire flowed into
China. During the past few years, 1,178 coins of the Sassanian dynasty or
Sassanian-Arabian type have been discovered in thirty-four finds (fig. 76).
The Sassanian coins belong to different periods over an interval of about
350 years from Shapur II (310–79) to Yazdegerd III (632–51), the last
king of the Sassanian dynasty. Most of the coins have been unearthed
either along the Silk Road or along the routes which stretched from Xi'an
at its eastern end to such capitals as Wuqia, Kuche, and Turfan in Xinjiang;
Xining, Qinghai; Xi'an and Yao County, Shaanxi; Shan County and
Luoyang, Henan; Datong and Taiyuan, Shanxi; and Ding County, Hebei.

92

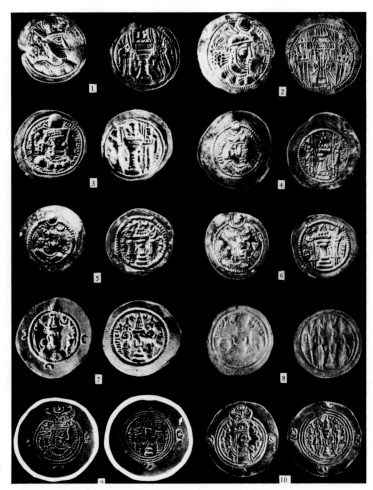

76 Sassanian silver coins found in China

Those found in the tombs of the Southern Dynasties in Guandong Province were probably imported by sea. Some dozen gold coins of the Eastern Roman Empire have been found in Hetian and Turfan in Xinjiang, Xi'an, Zanhuang County in Hebei, and Bike Qi in Inner Mongolia and cover a long period of about two hundred years from Constantine II (337–40) to Heraclius (610–41). Imported gold and silver coins were used for different purposes. Those found among the hoards in Wuqia and Xining were probably personal property buried for safety; those buried under the pagoda foundations in Ding and Yao Counties were religious offerings; and those found in the tombs were the money either placed in the mouth of the deceased or used as ornamental pendants with a hole.

77 Epitaph of the wife of Su Liang (Suren) unearthed in Xi'an. Upper half written in Pahlavi and lower half in Chinese

Finally, a word about the bilingual epitaph in Chinese and Pahlavi which was excavated at Xi'an. It is the epitaph of a Mrs. Su née Ma (849–74), the wife of Su Liang (Suren in Persian), a believer in Zoroastrianism (fig. 77). Su Liang was a member of the nobility in the Sassanian dynasty. His predecessors came in exile in China when Persia was invaded by the Arabs in 642. During the reign of Zhenyuan (787), the Tang dynasty incorporated into its own forces thousands of people from the Western Regions who lived in exile in Chang'an. It was at this time that his forefathers were appointed Honorary Commanders of the Left Sacred Strategy Army, and Su Liang in turn inherited the title. The Pahlavi language or Middle Persian came into use in the Parthian dynasty and was predominant under the Sassanian dynasty. The epitaph is inscribed in the cursive writing of the latest period of the Pahlavi script, a script created by the Zoroastrians. It constitutes not only a valuable philological document but also a typical and precious historical relic of the cultural exchange between China and the West.

94

23. Investigations and Excavations in the City of Dadu of the Yuan Dynasty

Dadu, the capital of the Yuan dynasty (1271–1368), now the city of Beijing, was constructed in 1267 and became one of the world-famous metropolises of the time. The Italian traveller Marco Polo described Dadu as "Khanbalik" (the city of the Khan or Emperor) and praised it as being well planned, beautiful, and prosperous.

Archaeological research on Yuan dynasty Dadu started in 1964 and was brought to a temporary halt in 1974. During those ten years, investigations of its walls, streets, rivers, and lakes were carried out, some dozen residential quarters and buildings of different types were excavated, and large quantities of articles for daily use and other relics were unearthed. All this has presented a better picture of the layout of this famous city, its architectural styles and techniques, and the life of the local people of different social strata.

The outer walls of Dadu were built of rammed earth. Its northern wall is still standing. The whole city is shaped like a rectangle with a perimeter of 28,600 metres. There were eleven gates (fig. 78), four of which were in use right up to the Ming and Qing dynasties. When the Xizhi Gate of the early Ming period was demolished in the summer of 1969, the west outer gateway of the barbican of the Hoyi Gate, a relic of Dadu, was brought to light (fig. 79). The Hoyi Gate was built in 1358, and its height as preserved is 22 metres, with a gateway 9.92 metres deep by 4.62 metres wide. This gateway was covered over by brick facings in the early Ming period, and the whole Hoyi Gate was renamed the Xizhi Gate. The fire-extinguishing equipment specially made to safeguard the gate could still be seen on the tower during the excavation.

The Imperial Palace and the Imperial City are situated south of the city centre. A main street running from north to south, through the middle of the palace, was discovered during the excavation and has proved to be the main axial line of Dadu. This has rectified the original hypothesis that the axial line of Dadu was slightly to the west.

The streets of Dadu are well planned. Basically its main streets run from north to south and are crossed by smaller lanes, parallel to and equidistant from each other, running from east to west. Even today, many streets and lanes of the inner city of Beijing still conform to this pattern. Marco Polo was perfectly right in saying that the streets were "in parallel lines" and "as orderly as a chessboard."

A scientific exploration has been made of the sites of the Haizi Lake, the Tonghui River, and the Jinshui River which run through the whole

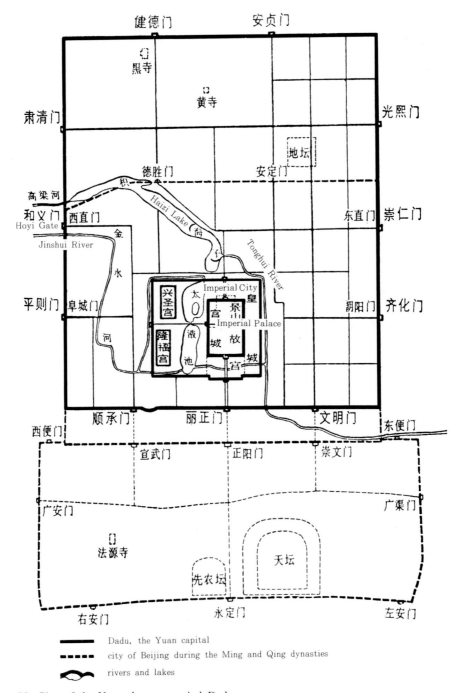

健德门　　　安贞门

黑寺

黄寺

肃清门　　　　　　　　　　　　光熙门

地坛

德胜门　　安定门

高梁河
积

Haizi Lake
荷

和义门
西直门　　　　　　　　　　　东直门　崇仁门
Hoyi Gate
Jinshui River

金
水

Tonghui River

平则门　阜城门　　　　　　　　　　　朝阳门　齐化门

兴圣宫
太
液
池

Imperial City
皇
宫
景
城
故
宫
Imperial Palace

隆福宫

河

顺承门　　　丽正门　　　　文明门　　东便门

西便门

宣武门　　　正阳门　　　崇文门

广安门　　　　　　　　　　　　广渠门

法源寺

天坛

先农坛

右安门　　　永定门　　　　左安门

———　 Dadu, the Yuan capital
- - - - -　 city of Beijing during the Ming and Qing dynasties
～～～　 rivers and lakes

78　Plan of the Yuan dynasty capital Dadu

96

79 Barbican of the Hoyi Gate remains of Dadu, present-day Beijing

80 Residential site of Dadu, present-day Beijing

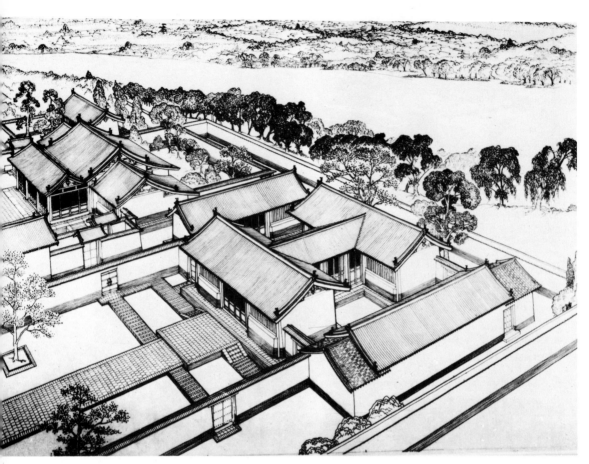

81 Sketch of residential site in Dadu

city. The use of archaeological methods has for the first time revealed the course of the Jinshui River, of which there was no clear account in historical records. The culverts under the city walls have also been excavated.

Of more than ten residential sites excavated, that near the present Houyingfang Lane is the most important. This is the site of a big building with the main hall of the principal courtyard built on a platform base. The house has a porch in front and a projecting annex behind (fig. 80). In the eastern courtyard stands an I-shaped building. A corridor links the rooms in the north and those in the south. This is the most popular pattern in the constructions of the Song and Yuan dynasties (fig. 81).

98

82 Flattened bottle of blue-and-white porcelain unearthed in Dadu, present-day Beijing

The house owners seem to have been forced to leave in such a hurry that many precious objects, such as chalcedony chessmen, rock crystal, ink-stone from Duanxi, and lacquerware inlaid with mother-of-pearl as well as blue-and-white porcelain, were left behind. Over two hundred chessmen made out of red and white chalcedony were scattered all over the floor of the main hall. From this one can imagine how alarmed and bewildered the owners were in their sudden departure.

Porcelain ware constitutes the majority of the relics unearthed in the residential sites. The porcelain used in Dadu is mostly Cizhou black-and-white decorated ware, Longquan celadon ware, Jingdezheng Yingqing ware of the Shufu type, and Northern Jun ware. The blue-and-white porcelain unearthed is small in quantity since it was very precious at that time. Some dozen pieces of blue-and-white porcelain found in a hoard boast a high artistic level both in shape and glaze (fig. 82). In addition, a Yingqing statuette of Guanyin (Avalokitesvara) and a big Jun-ware glazed vase (pl. 19) are among the rare fine porcelain objects of the Yuan dynasty which have been discovered.

24. Excavation of Tombs from the Ming Dynasty

Of the archaeological discoveries from the Ming dynasty (1368–1644), the tombs are the most important. In the past thirty years, the number of tombs of emperors, princes, and nobles from the Ming dynasty excavated throughout the country has reached about one hundred. The following is a brief account of the three most famous tombs.

In 1970 the tomb of Zhu Tan, the prince of Lu, was excavated at the southern foot of Mount Jiulong in Zou County, Shandong. Zhu Tan died in 1389. As water had accumulated inside the tomb, most of the grave-goods were in a good state of preservation when unearthed. They include a crown with nine strings of beads, leather caps, caps of black gauze with two upturned wings, and silk and cotton clothing of different kinds, as well as a quantity of lacquer furniture, of which one piece of gold-inlaid lacquerware is a rare specimen. A zither made in 1164 was already 225 years old when it was buried with Zhu Tan and was still in good condition when excavated. Of great interest to us are three scrolls of silk paintings and seven sets of block-printed books of the Yuan dynasty. In the three scrolls of paintings, there is a painting in gold of Blossoming Hibiscus and Butterflies with an inscription by Emperor Gaozong of the Song dynasty, and a painting of white lotus done by Qian Zuan of the Yuan dynasty. Among the seven sets of block-printed books, six rare editions have never been recorded before; two of them, for example, are the *Book of Documents Annotated by Cai (Caishi shu zhuanji)*, with six *juan* bound in three volumes in the butterfly style, and the *Poems of Du Fu (Du Gongbu shishi)*, with thirty-six *juan* bound in two volumes—a block-printed edition of 1287.

The tomb of Zhu Yuelian, the eldest son of the prince of Shu, was excavated in 1970 in Chengdu, Sichuan Province. He was buried in 1410. The tomb is a large and magnificent brick and stone construction, composed of three brick barrel vaults. It is 33 metres long and consists of a front door, a front courtyard, a second door, a principal courtyard, a main hall, a middle courtyard, a round hall, and a rear hall as well as two wing-rooms and two side-rooms on either side—an exact copy of the then royal palace. The doors, halls, corridors, and side-rooms are built with big stones and glazed tiles. As the tomb had been robbed long before, most of the grave-goods of value had disappeared. However, more than five hundred glazed-pottery guard-of-honour figurines, height 31–32 centimetres, were lined up in order in front of the wing-rooms flanking the principal and middle courtyards (fig. 83). They included armour-clad warriors, attendants carrying flags and weapons, and musicians playing

83 Tomb chamber of Zhu Yuelian's tomb from the Ming dynasty and its guard-of-honour figurines unearthed in Chengdu, Sichuan

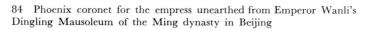

84 Phoenix coronet for the empress unearthed from Emperor Wanli's Dingling Mausoleum of the Ming dynasty in Beijing

various instruments. A few figurines of attendants were serving in the rear hall. The figurines are shaped so skilfully that they are all lifelike. Pottery royal carriages, reduced to scale, are modelled with careful attention to detail.

Lastly, we should make mention of the Dingling Mausoleum in Beijing ("Underground Palace"), the tomb of Emperor Wanli of the Ming dynasty who was buried in 1620. The excavation of the Dingling Mausoleum started in May 1957 and came to an end in July 1957. The mausoleum is composed of five roomy stone-built halls. It measures 97 metres in length from the entrance to the rear wall. The front, middle, and rear halls each have a finely carved stone door. Over three thousand funeral objects were unearthed there. Gold and silver vessels, elegant porcelain and jade articles, a variety of clothing, and bolts of silk brocade were among the art treasures which were discovered. The gold crown of the emperor and the phoenix coronet of the empress are the most outstanding relics unearthed there. The gold crown is minutely woven out of gold threads, and the phoenix coronet is inlaid with more than five thousand pearls and over one hundred precious stones (fig. 84). Both of them are dazzlingly brilliant. The Dingling Mausoleum has now become an underground museum, a world-famous place for cultural study and sightseeing.

A Brief Chinese Chronology

Primitive Society	ca. 700,000–4,000 years ago
Xia	21st–16th century B.C.
Shang	16th–11th century B.C.
Western Zhou	11th century–771 B.C.
Eastern Zhou	
Spring and Autumn Period	770–476 B.C.
Warring States Period	475–221 B.C.
Qin	221–207 B.C.
Western Han	206 B.C.–A.D. 24
Eastern Han	25–220
The Three Kingdoms	220–265
Western Jin	265–316
Eastern Jin	317–420
Southern and Northern Dynasties	420–589
Sui	581–618
Tang	618–907
Five Dynasties	907–960
Liao	916–1125
Song	960–1279
Jin	1115–1234
Yuan	1271–1368
Ming	1368–1644
Qing	1644–1911
Republic of China	1912–1949
People's Republic of China	1949–present

1 (*left*) Gourd-shaped painted pottery bottle unearthed at Jiangzhai, Lintong County, Shaanxi

2 (*right*) Painted pottery jar unearthed at Dadiwan, Qinan County, Gansu

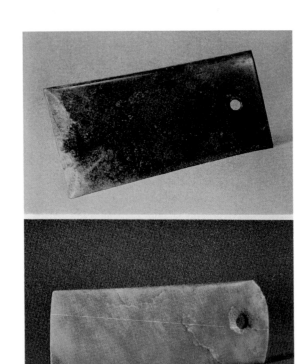

3 Jade spades unearthed at Dawenkou,
Taian County, Shandong

4 Large bronze tetrapod
unearthed in Zhengzhou,
Henan

5 Turquoise-inlaid ivory cup unearthed from Fu Hao's tomb
in Anyang, Henan

6 Half-feminine–half-masculine
jade figurine unearthed from
Fu Hao's tomb

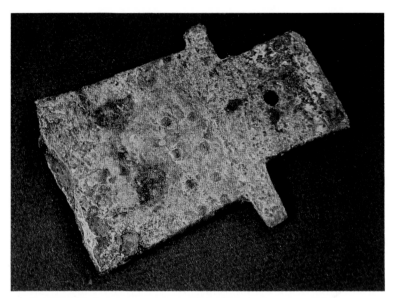

7 Iron-bladed bronze axe of the Shang dynasty found at Taixicun, Gaocheng County, Hebei

8 Painted wooden animal tomb guard unearthed from a Chu state tomb in Xinyang, Henan

9 Bronze chime-bells unearthed from the tomb of the Marquis Yi of Zeng in Sui County, Hubei

10 Vermilion-coloured gauze gown

*From Mawangdui Tomb 1
in Changsha, Hunan*

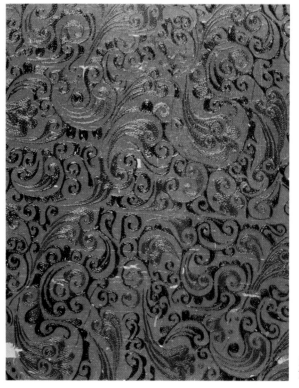

11 Yellow silk embroidered with the
longevity (*changshou*) pattern

From Mawangdui Tomb 1

12   Lacquerware pot (*hu*)

13   Lacquerware tray and plates

14 Silk painting unearthed from Mawangdui Tomb 1

15 *Boshan* incense burner with gold inlays unearthed from Mancheng Tomb 1 (Liu Sheng's tomb) of the Han dynasty in Hebei

16 Gilded bronze lamp with the inscription "Changxing Palace," unearthed from Mancheng Tomb 2 (Dou Wan's tomb)

17 Liu Sheng's jade suit unearthed from Mancheng Tomb 1

18   Wall painting of maids of honour from the tomb of Princess Yongtai in Qian County, Shaanxi

19 Jun-ware porcelain vase unearthed from the
Yuan dynasty capital Dadu, present-day Beijing

PRINCIPAL ARCHAE
PEOPLE'S REP

KUCHE

TURFAN

WUQIA

XINJIANG

GANSU

JIAYUGUAN

QINGHAI

XININ

XIZANG
(TIBET)

SICHUAN

YUANMOU

YUNNAN

0   300km

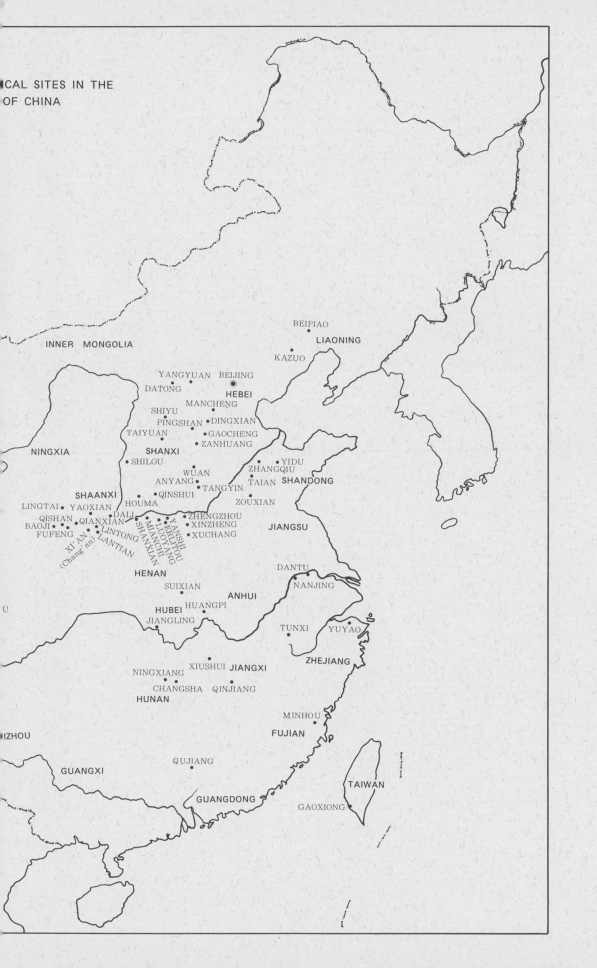

INNER MONGOLIA

BEIPIAO

LIAONING

KAZUO

YANGYUAN BEIJING

DATONG

HEBEI

MANCHENG

SHIYU

PINGSHAN DINGXIAN

TAIYUAN GAOCHENG

ZANHUANG

SHANXI

SHILOU

YIDU
ZHANGQIU

WUAN

ANYANG TAIAN SHANDONG

TANGYIN

QINSHUI

ZOUXIAN

SHAANXI

HOUMA

LINGTAI YAOXIAN

DALI ZHENGZHOU

QISHAN QIANXIAN XINZHENG

BAOJI XUCHANG

FUFENG LINTONG

XI'AN LANTIAN

(Chang'an)

YANSHI
ERLITOU
LUOYANG
MIANCHI
SHANXIAN

JIANGSU

HENAN

SUIXIAN DANTU

NANJING

ANHUI

HUANGPI

HUBEI

JIANGLING

TUNXI YUYAO

ZHEJIANG

XIUSHUI JIANGXI

NINGXIANG

CHANGSHA QINJIANG

HUNAN

MINHOU

FUJIAN

IZHOU

QUJIANG

GUANGXI

TAIWAN

GUANGDONG

GAOXIONG

NINGXIA